Pathfinder 40

Just write!

The *Pathfinder* Series

All **Pathfinders** are available through
good book suppliers or direct from:
Central Books, 99 Wallis Rd,
London E9 5LN. Tel: 0845 458 9910
(mail order line). Fax: 0845 458 9912.
Book trade representation (UK and
Ireland): **Broadcast Book Services,**
Charter House, 29a London Road, Croydon
CR0 2RE. Tel: 020 8681 8949.
Fax: 020 8688 0615.

Pathfinder 40

A CILT series for language teachers

Just write!

Julie Adams with Sally Ann Panter

Centre for Information
on Language Teaching and Research

The views expressed in this publication are the authors' and do not necessarily represent those of CILT, or any persons or organisations mentioned.

Acknowledgements

We would like to thank all the teachers and pupils who have generously shared their writing ideas with us, but in particular colleagues in the London Borough of Islington and from Haggerston School, Hackney. In addition, thanks go to Hana Cowan, George Green's School; Deborah Hillard, Brampton Manor School; Sandie Fillingham, Christ's College; Aude Lacroix, Wembley High School, Dr Wayne Luk, Imperial College; Karolina Mörnsjö; Dr Paco Rodriguez-Manas; Gous Uddin, South Camden Community School. Finally, we would like in a small way to commemorate the professionalism and creativity of the late Christine Neumayr whose 'Photo-Robot' idea is included on page 41.

First published 2001 by the Centre for Information on Language Teaching and Research (CILT), 20 Bedfordbury, London WC2N 4LB

ISBN 1 902031 50 4

A catalogue record for this book is available from the British Library

Printed in Great Britain by Copyprint UK Ltd

CILT Publications are available from: **Central Books,** 99 Wallis Rd, London E9 5LN. Tel: 0845 458 9910. Fax: 0845 458 9912. Book trade representation (UK and Ireland): **Broadcast Book Services,** Charter House, 29a London Road, Croydon CR0 2RE. Tel: 020 8681 8949. Fax: 020 8688 0615.

Contents

Introduction

'Written work' must be taught – only rarely does it happen incidentally. (Tainsh 1991: 3)

The teaching of writing currently has a high profile in the KS2 curriculum, where there is concern that levels of achievement in writing are below those in reading. This is reflected in secondary MFL, where it is not uncommon for pupils' scores to be lowest in writing of all the four skills.

In 2000, at the end of KS2, 83% of pupils gained Level 4 in reading, but only 55% in writing. This mismatch in skills is being addressed by extending the National Literacy Strategy (NLS) into KS3, and all staff will receive cross-curricular training on literacy. As part of the KS3 NLS there are six Literacy Progress Units aimed at providing extra support for pupils who need help to cope with the learning demands of the secondary curriculum. These six units are:

1 Writing organisation

2 Information retrieval

3 Spelling

4 Reading between the lines

5 Applying knowledge of phonics in writing

6 Sentence structure

These areas will be familiar to MFL teachers and link clearly to our curriculum. This book reflects renewed interest in the effective teaching of writing and we address much of the content covered in Literacy Progress Units 1, 3, 5 and 6.

Therefore, this book attempts to examine best practice and ways in which attainment in writing can be raised at least to the levels of other skills. As children often find writing the most difficult skill or enjoy it least, throughout we look at ways to motivate and support learners in their writing. We start off by looking at what theory and research tell us about learning to write in a foreign language.

1. Understanding writing

The traditional view of writing was that children needed to be taught a complex set of skills in strict sequence ... The research findings of recent years, however, point to a very different picture of what is involved in becoming a successful writer. ... Reading, writing, speaking and listening are interrelated – and not discrete – language skills. All four language skills are concerned with making meaning and children draw on existing knowledge in each mode for learning in the others. (Edwards 1995: 2)

There is no shortage of good ideas for writing tasks in the foreign language classroom, but what is needed to make these a success is more guidance for the MFL teacher on how to use such tasks to develop skills leading to good practice in writing. Swarbrick reminds us that as teachers of **foreign** languages we have a disadvantage:

Pupils do not have the facility to pluck language from the air as they might in their mother tongue. (Swarbrick 1994: 144)

Writing tasks and skills are often presented as falling into three distinct categories, which reflect the move from the pre-communicative to the communicative and very approximately correspond to the writing tasks at GCSE Foundation, 'overlap' and Higher tier levels.

SECRETARY	COMMUNICATOR	COMPOSER
Recording vocabulary Lists Taking notes	Messages Postcards Letters Posters	Stories Books Reports

This view of learning to write in three stages can be described in a variety of ways, each one implying that initially there is a greater focus on the medium, which gradually moves to a greater focus on the message (see table opposite).

The National Literacy Strategy talks about writing at:

* Word level
* Sentence level
* Text level

Therefore in Chapters 3, 4 and 5 we look at writing tasks for the foreign language classroom which suit each of these three stages.

CILT

Input	Practice	Use
The learner is introduced to an area of language	The learner is given an opportunity to rehearse areas of language	The learner is given real opportunities to use this language
Novice	Apprentice hack	Author
The learner writer is starting to learn basic skills	The learner writer can produce pieces of writing according to a template or model mostly to a standard format	The learner writer can write independently
Writing to learn	Writing to a model	Learning to write
The learner writer uses writing as a skill which helps him/her to learn the new language area	The learner writer can produce pieces of writing according to a template or model	The learner writer develops explicit skills which improve his/her writing

WRITING IN THE NATIONAL LITERACY STRATEGY

It is much clearer now that the cognitive skills associated with literacy are not acquired separately in different languages. (Edwards 1995: 17)

By the time pupils start their MFL studies in KS3, they have already been exposed to much good practice in the teaching of writing in other curriculum areas. Therefore, we are more likely to succeed in teaching MFL writing if we draw on similar approaches that children recognise and the skills they have been developing elsewhere. In KS2, pupils encounter a structured approach to learning how to write through the National Literacy Strategy (NLS).

The NLS aims to empower children by giving them control over their use of language for writing. It also seeks to deconstruct the language-learning process so that the skills and knowledge identified may be taught explicitly to children. While this structured approach is already familiar to teachers of modern languages, the NLS can provide the MFL teacher with ideas for improving writing skills. Examples include the use of texts as models for the study of different text types and the direct teaching of language features. The focus in the NLS on children understanding sentence structure also helps them to create language effects to enhance their writing.

The strategy aims to teach word, sentence and text level skills explicitly, to equip children with the skills and knowledge to make meanings and manipulate language to express their ideas. The NLS introduces pupils to the different stages of writing – planning, drafting and editing their work. Through 'guided writing' children are prepared for writing using listening, speaking and reading. Writing is also supported using writing frames and improved with focused teaching of the building blocks such as topic sentences and connectives. By studying different types of model texts pupils develop an awareness of how different text types are structured and learn to vary their own writing for different purposes and audiences.

A teaching sequence is suggested for teaching writing within the NLS. A lesson would typically start with a short lesson starter focused at word level on key language for the lesson. This is followed by 'shared reading' of a text, which involves the study of the text type and sentence-level activities based on the text to reinforce the sentence-level objective of the lesson. Then 'shared writing' follows. First, there is the 'demonstration' when the teacher models the process of writing. Then the whole class collaborates with the teacher to produce a text, which is called 'scribing'. This is followed by 'supported composition', when the children compose following the model and show their writing to the teacher. A further stage provides pupils with the opportunity to write independently or in a group using the sentence-level features taught. The lesson finishes with a plenary to review progress in the lesson.

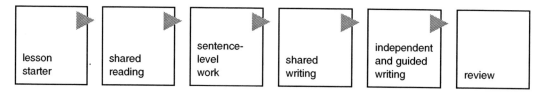

It is clear that the NLS reflects what is already best practice in MFL, and in later chapters we explore in more detail how these processes relate to the MFL classroom.

MATCHING SOUND TO PRINT

> *[KS4 pupils'] ability to work independently will be constrained by the difficulties they describe at word level to do with sounds, spellings and meaning, and further by the problems they have in making combinations of words work for them 'in the way Sir does', as one pupil memorably put it.* (Lee et al 1998: 59)

Matching sound to print is also called 'the association of the spoken and written form' and the NC calls it 'the interrelationship of sounds and writing'. It is a measure of the importance of this area that the NC makes it statement 1a of the Programme of Study! When we started to write this book we did not have a strong opinion on whether the written word should be introduced early or withheld as long as possible – we have seen teachers handle both approaches very well. However, in our reading we have found more published opinion and evidence that the written form should be introduced earlier rather than later:

CILT

Matching speech to writing [is] a problem which for many learners proves an insurmountable hurdle ... The teacher faces a dilemma. If he tries to shield the learner from the written form of the language, relying solely on the ear, the pupil is deprived of any support for the growing load on the memory. Pupils with limited short-term memory capacity have no means of reinforcing ear learning by eye learning in which at least half of an average class will be more confident and proficient. (Hawkins 1981: 83)

Opinions vary regarding the best time to introduce the written form of the language. There is no doubt that some learners, particularly those with poor auditory discrimination or poor memory for sounds, do benefit from an early association of sound and written forms. (McColl and Thomas 1997: Introduction)

For some students there will be a constant need to associate sound forms and text. It is likely to be a two-way process, with the one form supporting the learning of the other, compensating for memory weaknesses in one or other channel of communication. (McColl 2000: 41)

Whichever school of thought you personally subscribe to – or is borne out by your experience – it is very clear that it is vital that pupils experience an active and thorough introduction to the written form, regardless of when it is given. Most teachers acknowledge that matching sound to print is a particular challenge in French, but teachers of German, Spanish and Italian, for example, often underestimate the role that this plays. Look, for example, at the following letters which are significantly different from the sounds they represent in English writing:

- German   >   *ch | j | w | sch | z | ß | v*

- Spanish   >   *ll | v/b | c | qu*

- Italian   >   *gl | ci | z/zz | ch | ce | gg | gi*

We have found that where pupils have a very firm grasp of the sound system of the foreign language – from the first weeks of studying it – this helps them in their reading and writing. For example, it is much easier for an English speaker learning German to guess and/or remember that *Jahr* means year if they understand fully (and are reminded often) that J in German represents a Y sound. Teachers who teach a language with a different script, such as Russian or Gujerati, tend to approach the association of the spoken written forms with care, as the learners' difficulties with matching sound to print are more readily apparent. In fact, in all of the European languages and others using a Roman script, we have to teach accents which are unfamiliar to children who write only English. See Chapter 11 on teaching different scripts for helpful ideas of how to approach this.

Unfortunately, we often see in classrooms that the children have a full, active and interesting presentation of the oral/aural form of the language, but are merely given a vocabulary list of the written form of the new vocabulary, with no active presentation of the written form. McColl and Thomas suggest one approach:

When you feel that pupils are sufficiently confident of the sound, reveal the textual form of the word or phrase, saying it again as you do so, and asking them again to repeat. ... Repeat as often as necessary to make it clear that you are saying exactly the same, whether you show them the picture or the text. Ask them to repeat after you, showing them sometimes the text, sometimes the picture. (McColl and Thomas 1997)

For further practical suggestions on approaching this area see also the rhyming activities in Chapter 3 and 'Text and pronunciation', pages 2–4 in Pathfinder 21: *Creative use of texts* (Kavanagh and Upton 1994).

PITFALLS IN FOREIGN LANGUAGE WRITING

Writing tends to be the 'Cinderella' of the four skills (at least at the lower levels) and is often relegated to the end of the teaching unit and used mainly for homework. This is unlikely to make the learners want to write. (Byrne 1988: 28)

Before we start to look at effective practice in the teaching of writing, we would like to explore some common problems associated with writing we see in MFL classrooms. Swarbrick believes that a move to what is believed to be a more 'relevant' curriculum has narrowed the range of tasks:

In our attempt to link classroom interaction with the 'real' world outside the classroom, we have reduced that reality to a world of tourism where many loaves are bought and many predictable transactions take place but where no one tells a joke or a story. (Swarbrick 1994: 141)

Although many 'communicative' writing tasks (like the transactions Swarbrick describes above) at first appear to be authentic, often they lack any **real** purpose. Pupils write lots of plausible letters to non-existent penfriends, but less often write anything for a genuine audience or which they are realistically personally motivated to write. Unfortunately, this limited range of mostly unstimulating writing tasks is perpetuated in the GCSE terminal writing tests which mainly centre on letter writing or other kinds of correspondence and transactional tasks.

Writing, whether in the mother tongue or a second language, is a medium of communication that requires a range of skills, many of which are different to those employed in speech. Unlike speaking we have to be taught to write and we recognise that whilst offering benefits it imposes considerable constraints on the writer. It is not generally seen by the young or adults as a pleasurable activity in the mother tongue, and this is even less so in the second or foreign language. (Fowler 1989: 90)

Although the majority of foreign language teachers provide writing tasks for their pupils regularly, these are not always integrated with the other skills. Moreover, it is not uncommon to see teachers give pupils a task to 'do', with little or no guidance or preparation. Until recently, few coursebooks have taught explicit writing skills, and many also fell into the trap of providing writing tasks and leaving pupils to cope with them on their own. Nowadays, the best coursebooks

CILT

cover explicit skills development and give learners realistic support for producing a piece of extended writing as in the example from *Équipe 4* given on page 8.

Unfortunately, as teachers, we tend to exacerbate these problems by giving writing the reputation as the most difficult skill, reinforcing many pupils' beliefs that they just **can't** write. Also, writing tends to be treated consistently as a test with no opportunity to edit and draft or write in groups, and pupils' work is returned to them covered in red ink. In later chapters we describe approaches for encouraging even the most reluctant of writers, and also approaches to the marking of written work which avoid the overuse of negative feedback.

Although we started this section with a quote from Byrne outlining much of the problem with foreign language writing, he also goes on to give clues to possible solutions, which we will examine further in the next chapter:

> *Where possible, we should introduce writing activities that lead naturally onto or from the use of other skills, so that the learners see writing as a natural activity.*
> (Byrne 1988: 28)

Dossier: Est-ce que je suis en forme?

- write an essay on how fit you are
- use strategies for putting in more detail when writing or speaking

Est-ce que je suis en forme?
(300 mots)

1 introduction
2 développement
  a une journée typique; ce que je mange
  b l'exercice/le sport et moi; ce que j'ai
    fait récemment
  c mauvaises habitudes?
  d résolutions; ce que je vais faire
3 conclusion

Est-ce que je suis en forme?

par Sophie Castel

1 Pour être en forme, il faut bien manger et faire du sport. Il ne faut pas fumer et il ne faut pas aller au lit trop tard.

2a Moi, le matin, je me lève à sept heures et demie. Au petit déjeuner, je mange des céréales avec du lait et du sucre et je bois une tasse de thé. Je vais à l'école à pied tous les jours parce que la marche à pied, c'est bon pour la santé. A midi, je mange à la cantine. Je mange beaucoup de légumes mais je n'aime pas beaucoup le chou-fleur et je déteste les épinards. C'est dommage parce que les épinards contiennent beaucoup de vitamines. Quand je peux, je mange des fruits. Je pense que j'ai un régime équilibré. Le soir, je me couche toujours de bonne heure.

2b Au lycée, on joue au basket et au handball. Pendant mon temps libre, je fais aussi beaucoup de sport. Je fais du jogging tous les soirs et ça me détend. Je joue au tennis une fois par semaine et je fais du judo depuis l'année dernière. Quand je peux, je fais de la natation ou je fais du vélo. Samedi dernier, j'ai participé à un mini-marathon. J'ai couru dix kilomètres. C'était amusant mais j'avais mal aux pieds.

2c Je ne fume pas et je ne bois pas d'alcool, seulement un verre de vin une ou deux fois par mois. Je ne vais pas commencer à fumer parce que le tabac donne le cancer. J'ai une mauvaise habitude: je mange entre les
2d repas. J'aime manger du chocolat mais je vais essayer d'arrêter parce que ce n'est pas bon pour la santé. Il y a trop de calories et ça fait grossir.

3 Je ne suis pas souvent malade et je vais rarement chez le médecin. Pour moi, la santé est assez importante. J'essaie d'avoir une vie active et saine. Je pense que je suis en forme.

Source: Équipe 4 *by Bourdais, Finnie and Gordon (OUP, 2000)*

CiLT

2. Getting going with writing

A writing activity is very often the end product of a unit of work and this occurs naturally in our teaching progression. However, writing can be introduced earlier in a unit of work as a vehicle for completing a task in another skill, as happens continually with reading, for example. When writing is integrated with the other skills in this way it can encourage learners to take more risks with their writing, produce language more fluently or to write lengthier texts. This is probably because in such integrated tasks learners are concentrating more on the message than the medium.

For example, in this task Year 11 pupils were preparing to write an account of a holiday prompted by a picture story. Part of the preparation involved focusing on a spoken account of the picture story below that pupils recorded on tape.

Source: Teach yourself
GCSE French *by Hares*
(Hodder & Stoughton, 1987)

First of all, the key language to build up a picture story can be elicited through oral questioning by the teacher as a model in a whole-class grouping, which can then be written down and shared. In the next stage, the teacher first models changing the factual details and then gets pupils to practise this. Gradually, the teacher adds a variety of higher-level language features orally, e.g. pupils brainstorm adjectives and then add examples at sentence level to the account. In this way, pupils can be trained how to extend from the model. Structured extension training can be directed by the teacher using alternative questions with short written prompts and pictures to encourage pupils to recycle appropriate, familiar language. Here is an example of a visual prompt for describing a stay in a hotel.

Visual prompt examples

H ▶ ** ▶ "LE MANOIR"** + 🍸 + 🏋

➤ Nous sommes restés dans un <u>grand</u> hôtel quatre étoiles **qui** s'appelle Le Manoir **où** il y a un bar <u>très chic</u> et un gymnase <u>moderne</u>.

This can then be followed up by pupils writing their own transcript for the speaking task. By making a recording in this way, pupils can focus on their ideas without feeling self-conscious about the accuracy of their writing. If a written task is set subsequently, pupils can be encouraged to work from the transcript they have already produced. Pupils can then concentrate on editing their own work and focusing on accuracy.

A MULTI-SKILL APPROACH TO WRITING

We need to integrate writing with the other skills so pupils are adequately prepared for each writing task. Two approaches which encourage this integration of skills are known as 'language experience' and 'process writing'. Language experience is defined as being designed for 'use in the early stages' (Edwards 1995: 5) but elements of this approach will be familiar to most foreign language teachers: the teacher discusses a topic with pupils and then offers support, such as providing relevant vocabulary to get the children started on their writing. On the other hand, process writing is the approach found in the National Curriculum for English:

> *Process writing takes place in classrooms where real writing is given a high priority, where children are given a range of reasons for writing and work in an atmosphere which encourages collaboration and mutual support.* (Edwards 1995: 6)

CILT

The six main steps of process writing are: rehearsal, drafting, responding to writing (sharing in groups), revision, editing and publishing. This is a practice that can easily be replicated in the foreign language classroom by allowing pupils to write in pairs and groups, and preparing for the writing task through the other skills. This contrasts with the view of writing presented by Byrne in Chapter 1 where writing is divorced from the other skills.

Moreover, it is important to develop specific writing skills in our pupils. Most teachers share with their pupils the advice that it is essential to include 'tenses and opinions' in their writing (and speaking) if pupils are to have access to Grade C and above at GCSE level. Unfortunately, many pupils do not understand what this means, in the same way that they do not really understand what is meant by a piece of writing having a 'beginning, a middle and an end'. Therefore, in Chapter 6 we look at developing appropriate skills for writing, and in Chapters 4 and 5 we look at learning to structure writing.

WRITING GAMES

One way to integrate writing naturally with the other skills is to use games involving writing. Sometimes these can be games already well known in the MFL classroom, but with a written element added. Here are some examples of games which integrate writing well with the other skills and focus on expanding pupils' use of a range of language.

'ADD A WORD 1'

Add an appropriate word (in any position) to the phrase which has already been written. This game works particularly well if each new word is written on a large Post-It note so that the word order can be changed, or it can also be directed by the teacher who writes pupils' suggestions onto the board or OHP.

> ^ Je suis allé ^ au cinéma ^
>
> *hier*　　　　　　　*lentement*　　　　　*parce que ...*

'ADD A WORD 2'

Each group writes a sentence on large paper and cuts it into separate words; these word cards are then passed on to the next group, which has to reassemble the sentence and adds another word card to the sentence. Then cards are passed on to the next group again. (The teacher could prompt by suggesting what to add at each round, e.g. a time marker, an adverb, an adjective.)

'ADD A WORD PLUS'

The teacher writes a sentence on the board/OHP. Pupils then have to invent the sentence which comes before or after this sentence.

'I'M SORRY, I HAVEN'T A CLUE'

The teacher starts a sentence and each group/person must add a word to the end – the object is to keep the sentence going as long as possible (link words, of course, are particularly advantageous here). Although this game can be played orally, it is more helpful in developing writing skills if the teacher scribes the sentence on the board or OHP as pupils dictate each word.

'FONDANT FANCIES'

The teacher gives each group a starter sentence and challenges them to make it as long/complex/ fancy as possible.

'ÉCONOMIQUE AVEC LA VÉRITÉ'

The teacher prepares an exaggerated description, report or account, which pupils must then change to the truth (or vice versa). Iain Mitchell suggests a similar idea where pupils have to read holiday brochures (for example) to find the language which attempts to make the destination sound as attractive as possible. This activity could precede 'Économique avec la vérité'.

'SENSE AND SENSIBILITY'

Change nonsense sentences into something sensible (or vice versa); this is particularly good for practising dull transactional topics.

'MEMORY MOMENT'

The teacher reads out a list of vocabulary once. Pupils then have 30 seconds to write down as much of the vocabulary they can remember; this is useful in recapping vocabulary from former units, particularly in KS4.

CILT

3. Focus on word level

Pupils need to learn to write from the beginning of their language education:

- to help them remember the new language by supporting the other skills;
- to learn the written conventions of the foreign language;
- to experience a sense of achievement.

Generally, foreign language teachers in this country tend to be good at such 'word-level' work, and we have many creative ideas for getting beginner learners to write individual words and short phrases. However, sometimes we resort too readily to the option of creating illustrated dictionaries, especially for lower-ability learners, who aren't necessarily any better at drawing than any other pupils are. Acrostics are a good example of a successful 'word-level' activity. These allow pupils to be creative and to respond to the task according to their ability. Some pupils will find single words which cross the 'key' word at any point, others will work hard to find a word which begins with each initial letter of the key word, while some might even construct whole sentences. For example, using PARIS as the 'key' word.

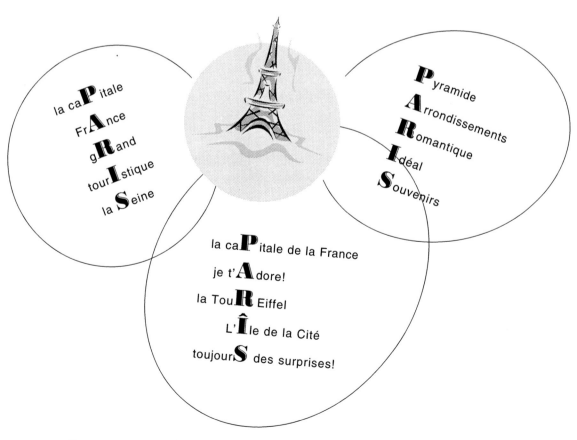

la ca**P**itale
Fr**A**nce
g**R**and
tour**I**stique
la **S**eine

Pyramide
Arrondissements
Romantique
Idéal
Souvenirs

la ca**P**itale de la France
je t'**A**dore!
la Tou**R** Eiffel
L'**Î**le de la Cité
toujour**S** des surprises!

Copying lists of vocabulary can be useful in helping to start to create a 'kinaesthetic' sense of the word, but if this is really to help pupils remember the language, they need to write each word more than once. In the research study *The invisible child* which surveyed Year 9 pupils, 'copying from the board or from a book' achieved by far the highest score as being an activity which doesn't help pupils to learn, 'mainly on the grounds that it is done as an unthinking process with no personal involvement and does not promote retention or understanding' (Lee *et al* 1998: 29). Copying was also the second least popular activity. Lee *et al* place particular emphasis on this point:

> It is important to note that pupils readily distinguish between whether they like/dislike an activity and whether they find it helpful or not. They do not make a simplistic connection: vocabulary tests, for example, attract a fairly high unpopularity score but also score quite well on helpfulness. (ibid 1998: 30)

So why do we spend so much time doing an activity (copying lists of words) which pupils both dislike and find unhelpful in the learning process? Almost certainly because there is a challenge at this level in devising tasks which are interesting and intrinsically worthwhile, but need only a small amount of language to complete them. To paraphrase Tony Blair, what we need at this stage is 'Repetition, Repetition, Repetition!'. HMI agrees that simple writing tasks still need to be stimulating:

> At the earliest stage ... it is desirable that copying should entail some selection and discrimination on the part of pupils and not be a mindless activity. (HMI 1987: 22)

Therefore, in this chapter we focus on activities which can be tackled by beginners in the foreign language, mainly at 'word level', but which are still motivating and worthwhile.

 IDEAS FOR SMALL AMOUNTS OF LANGUAGE

CODES

The use of codes and ciphers requires pupils to copy words and sentences. However, the fact that these words are embedded in a code provides a **reason** for copying out the words and some degree of motivation in 'cracking' the code. Codes and ciphers have to be handled with care in the early stages of foreign language learning – pupils are already having to 'decode' a new form of language, so jumbling these new words can add a further level of difficulty. For this reason it is usually best to avoid codes which are substitutions of one letter for another, e.g. A becomes Z, B becomes Y, C becomes X, etc. Instead, here are suggestions using a variety of other symbols to substitute for letters. These suggestions are probably not suitable for pupils with literacy difficulties, unless you are sure that they enjoy and benefit from 'code-breaking' activities. One word of advice – an easy extension activity is to ask pupils to invent their own codes. If you do so, ask them also to decode their encoded message before submitting to you, or even better swap with a partner to get them to decode it.

cilt

SECRET AGENT

This is the kind of activity which is actually more difficult to explain than to do! When we have used this with pupils we have mostly distributed the worksheet without explanation and challenged them to 'crack the code'. However, if you need help in working it out ... each shape matches a shape in the key grid surrounding the letter. Find the matching shape, and see which letter it represents. For example, S =⟨⟩. The first two letters have been provided for you (answer on p80).

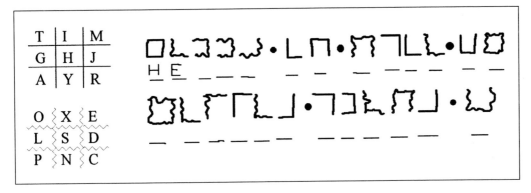

NUMBER CODES

Numerals lend themselves easily to code making. Each number can substitute either just one letter or a word, with the number allocated arbitrarily to a letter or word (only partial grid shown here).

1	2	3	4	5	6	7	8	9	10	11	12	13	14
e	p	l	i	d	n	k	j	s	c	o	f	t	g

4/3.4.7.1/ 10.11.5.1.9 = I like codes

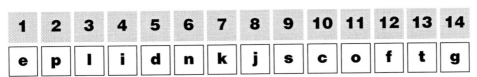

1	2	3	4	5	6	7	8	9
j'	je	n'	pas	le	la	aime	c'est	français

1.7/5/9 = j'aime le français

Both of these code-breaking tasks can be made more difficult if the numerals are replaced by the numbers written out in full in the target language. For example, the previous message becomes:

un.sept/cinq/neuf

PICTORIAL CODES

An easy way to create codes using symbols is to use symbol fonts on a word-processor. To do this write your message in a word-processing package, using double line spacing and a large point size. Now select the entire text and change to 'Wingdings' font (or a similar set of pictorial symbols), e.g. XYZ becomes . Now write out the alphabet once in the symbol font and once in the normal font to use as a key. This task can also be made more complex by withholding the key (or parts of it) from pupils and requiring them to guess what the words might be. You could also print out a copy of your original message in normal font to use as a self-access answer sheet.

If you have access to Camsoft's *Fun with texts* software, this kind of activity can be created even more easily using the 'Enigma' game in this software package (see p59 for a description of *Fun with texts*).

MINIMALIST POSTCARDS

These postcards are now common in holiday resorts. If pupils use them just by ticking their own choices, this is more a reading task than a writing task. To make this into a writing task, pupils could be encouraged to compile lists of possible answers under headings nominated by the teacher.

Source: Trojaborgs Forlag

POETRY FOR BEGINNERS

With an appropriate structure poetry writing in the foreign language can be made accessible even to beginner learners. Most of all pupils need to be encouraged that poems don't have to rhyme.

Bonjour les magasins.
Au revoir mon argent.

Guten Tag Schule.
Tschüss, meine Freizeit.

Привет телевизор,
До свидания работа.

The 'Hello, goodbye!' poem, originally invented by teachers in Cambridgeshire, is now familiar to most language teachers. This 'pattern poem' and similar ones are clever, as they require pupils to use only a noun to produce a witty piece of writing. Pupils can either work individually or contribute their lines to a longer poem. Even in the early stages poetry can be used to expand learners' use of grammar, as in this idea from Alison Taylor:

- Yesterday I was …
- Today I am …
- Tomorrow I will be …

Here are some other ideas we invented for pattern poems:

- *À bas …! Vive …!*　　　　　　*Nieder mit …! Es lebe …!*
  À bas les ados! Vive les profs!　　*Nieder mit der Schule! Es lebe die Freizeit!*

- No thanks … yes please.
  Atomkraft? Nein danke! Umwelt? Ja bitte!

- Hell is …, heaven is …!
  Hölle ist Sauerkraut, Himmel ist Schokolade!

TONGUE TWISTERS

Tongue twisters are a good way of encouraging pupils to focus on the form of language, in a way which is enjoyable. To prepare for this task, pupils have to find words in given categories beginning with a particular letter of the alphabet, e.g. *prénom, ville, animal, adjectif*. They then write these out as tongue twisters, e.g.

- *Sam habite en Espagne avec sept souris.*
- *Liesl und elf lange Lindenwürmer wohnen in Leipzig.*

Lily habite Lille
avec un lapin
et des lézards

PAR CRAIG ADAMS

If pupils enjoy this task you can find authentic tongue twisters in a wide variety of languages at www.uebersetzung.at/twister.

Source: Central Foundation Boys School, Islington

OCTO-POEMS

In this idea from Alison Taylor, pupils have to find a word in each of eight categories to describe a member of their family, e.g. a colour, a piece of furniture, an item of clothing, a hobby, a season, an item of food … The categories can be any area of language known to the pupils.

- My grandmother is pink.
- My grandmother is an armchair.
- My grandmother is a cardigan.
- My grandmother is knitting.
- My grandmother is autumn.
- My grandmother is rice pudding.
- My grandmother is …
- My grandmother is …

RHYMING POEMS

> *From an early age children make up rhymes … Children enjoy playing with words, particularly the kind of play which involves repetition.* (Beard 1995)

Rhymes are particularly difficult in a foreign language, as learners have a much smaller store of vocabulary to draw on than in their mother tongue. However, rhymes are very good for learning and practising pronunciation. Some children will only be able to approach such activities as reading tasks (e.g. matching words), but many more will build on the teacher's original idea and find their own rhymes. Sandy Brownjohn, children's poet and teacher of writing, suggests some alternatives to rhyme:

CILT

- Repetition – 'Polly put the kettle on'.
- Single word repetition – 'There was a crooked man'.
- Half (part or near) rhyme – 'Oranges and lemons'.
- Assonance – 'Little Bo Peep'.
- Consonance – the repeated sound within words near each other in the poem, which may or not occur at the ends of lines – 'Hickory dickory dock'.
- Alliteration – 'Sing a song of sixpence'.

(Brownjohn 1995: 80)

The following poem produced by a Year 3 teacher in Moscow demonstrates many examples of the above. I have used it with my pupils to practise reading and challenged them to find where the rhymes (or part rhymes) are (see p80 for a transliteration of the poem, and work out the 'across' and 'end of line' rhyming patterns for yourself).

As we discussed on page 6, rhymes can be particularly useful in helping pupils to associate the spoken and written forms of new language. There are several good examples of this kind of activity in coursebooks, such as this one from *Génial 1:*

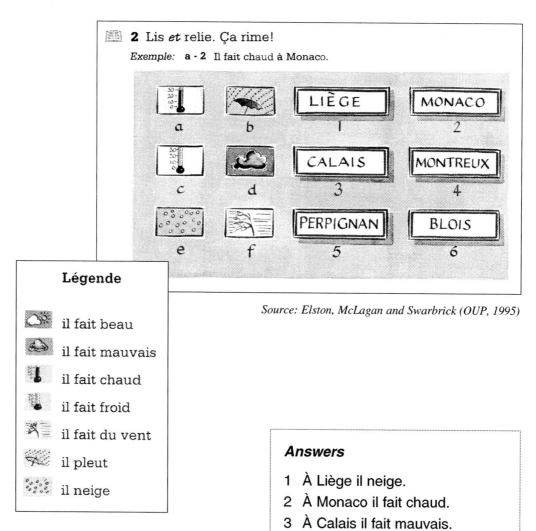

Source: Elston, McLagan and Swarbrick (OUP, 1995)

Légende

il fait beau

il fait mauvais

il fait chaud

il fait froid

il fait du vent

il pleut

il neige

Answers

1 À Liège il neige.
2 À Monaco il fait chaud.
3 À Calais il fait mauvais.
4 À Montreux il pleut.
5 À Perpignan il fait du vent.
6 À Blois il fait froid.

CiLT

Turn simple statements into a *comptine* or counting rhyme by using a nonsense word like this example from *Auto 1* (Buckby and Huntley, 1992), which changes the ending of the nonsense word each time to match the ending of the final word in the sentence:

Ramigrana au cinéma, Ramigrané a la télé ... Ramigranu tu as perdu!

Try these rhyming couplets yourself and see if you can guess the missing word each time (answers on p80):

- *Je m'appelle George, j'ai mal à la gorge.*
- *Je m'appelle Clément, j'ai mal aux ...*

(Haggerston School, Hackney)

- *Pat étudie les maths.*
- *Florence étudie les ...*

(Caroline Chevalier-Riffard, Northumberland Park Community School, Haringey)

Animal rhymes: *Le serpent est intelligent.*
                 L'eléphant est ...

RECIPES

Children are familiar with the format of recipes, and by adding nouns to a format prepared by the teacher, can create amusing pieces of writing:

Take _____
Add _____
Mix _____
Leave _____
And you have _____

RECIPE FOR A TEACHER
Take one dictionary
Add a red biro
Mix with a loud voice
Leave in a classroom
And you have a teacher!

Overleaf in an example of a recipe being used at a more advanced level with KS4 pupils.

Une recette poétique!

1 Lis ce poème au sujet d'une personne sympa.
Souligne le vocabulaire des recettes utilisé dans le poème.
Cherche les mots que tu ne connais pas dans le dictionnaire.

> Les poèmes sont difficiles à écrire. Mais tu peux suivre un modèle pour le faire plus simplement. Voici un poème basé sur une recette.

> Prenez une personne,
> Ajoutez un bon esprit,
> Et un cœur gentil,
> Mélangez ensemble.
>
> Prenez une tête qui réfléchit bien,
> Une voix qui calme, et
> Ajoutez un rayon de bonheur.
> Mélangez,
> Et voilà une personne SYMPA.

Une recette pour une personne sympa, William Makower, Alastair Dant et James Gill, Netherhall School, Cambridge

2 Pense aux qualités d'une personne sympa.

a Fais une liste d'adjectifs pour décrire ce genre de personne.

☞ *agréable, rigolo, ...*

b Fais une liste des verbes qu'on utilise dans une recette.

☞ *tournez, mélangez, ajoutez, ...*

3 Ecris un poème «Une recette pour un meilleur ami/une meilleure amie».

TIP TIP **TIP** TIP **TIP** TIP **TIP**
- Keep your poem simple. Think about the idea of setting it out like a recipe. It needn't be long and it needn't rhyme.

★ Ecris un poème sous la forme d'une recette mais sur un thème totalement différent, comme la liberté, la guerre ou la paix.

Source: ALL French writing activities for KS4 by Swarbrick, Calvert and Gordon (ALL, 1997)

CiLT

4. Focus on sentence level

Writing is not just about getting words down on paper. They also have to be in the right order, with the right punctuation to guide your reader, and the right amount of detail to clarify your message. To do this you must be aware of the patterns of written language. (Palmer 2000: 13)

On page 3 we talked about 'beginner writers' going on to become 'apprentice hacks'. In the newspaper context this means a very junior journalist who has to produce formulaic items such as reports on weddings, football matches, school concerts and local council meetings, usually adhering reasonably closely to a tried and tested formula. In the foreign language classroom this is the stage at which pupils move on from writing words, phrases and isolated sentences, to combining these elements into short pieces of writing. Substitution exercises and gap-fill writing tasks are regularly used at this stage. These are helpful in developing writing skills in the foreign language as they show the learner how the words can be 'put together' to form authentic text. Many teachers worry that such structuring of writing is actually 'spoon-feeding', but HMIs agree with us that effective teaching of writing includes a phase of tight structuring:

For many pupils, independent writing of a simple kind can be introduced from the first year. If it is to be comprehensible to a native reader, it needs to be guided for a long time by the teacher rather than created by the pupil, though pupils can be encouraged to select and order what they want to write. (HMI 1987: 23)

There is nothing so terrifying as a blank canvas. (Picasso)

Many teachers of writing talk about the 'fear of the blank page' and obviously models of writing can help to remove this danger, as much of the text is already provided for the writer, who just has to personalise and complete it. However, models are not the universal panacea they seem at first:

- Models can be boring.
- Models can be too restrictive.
- Models can imply there is only one 'correct' way to do each writing task.
- Some models are too complex to allow the learner to see how the text has been constructed.

Some of these problems are illustrated in the following piece of work which was used as a piece of controlled conditions GCSE coursework for Year 10 pupils:

Controlled conditions coursework: Les vacances.

Lis la lettre de Michel. Ecris ta réponse, en changeant les mots soulignés. Si tu veux, ajoute des détails et des opinions.

Lundi, 25 juillet.

Cher Jean,

Mon école, le Collège Emile Zola, a fini samedi. J'ai huit semaines de vacances. Je suis à Cap d'Agde au sud de la France. Je suis dans un hôtel avec mon frère. L'hôtel s'appelle "Le Sable d'Or". Notre chambre est assez grande. Dans la ville, il y a un parc d'attractions et une belle plage. Il fait très chaud. Dimanche, ,j'ai visité la cathédrale. C'était intéressant. Ce soir je vais danser à la discothèque. C'est génial! Vendredi, on rentre à Paris.

A bientôt,

Michel.

This model was far too restrictive for many of the pupils, as it did not allow them to use other relevant language they had learnt – two pupils added phrases such as '*L'année dernière je suis allé en France*' after the end of the letter! Also, in the coursework context tasks such as these achieve quite low scores, as pupils are writing mainly nouns, or only very short phrases. The two pupils who added '*L'année dernière …*' demonstrated clearly that they would be capable of writing more if given a suitable task.

The challenge at this level of writing development, therefore, becomes providing writers with a 'scaffold' for their writing, rather than a 'straitjacket'. For example, when pupils are studying a unit of work where they will have to write a letter to a tourist office, the teacher can introduce a variety of different forms for starting and finishing a business letter via preparatory reading or listening activities.

STRUCTURING WRITING WITH WRITING FRAMES

One way to 'scaffold' writing which is now becoming familiar across the curriculum (particularly in KS2 and KS3) is by using a 'writing frame'. Writing frames are described in the National Literacy Strategy as: 'a structured prompt to support writing'. A writing frame usually consists of a series of boxes with a 'sentence starter' in the target language. Once these boxes are filled in, they produce a piece of continuous writing. Whereas worksheets usually provide practice of individual elements of new language, a writing frame brings several language items together to make a coherent text. Gap-fill exercises provide more structure than writing frames and are a way of guiding language use, i.e. how to manipulate a particular structure. By contrast, frames allow writers to add their own ideas and language to make a piece of continuous text.

In this writing frame from *French writing frames: Personal feelings and opinions* (Adams 2000*b*) we can see how pupils have been supported with the helpsheet to use the simple future tense with common vocabulary to state their New Year resolutions.

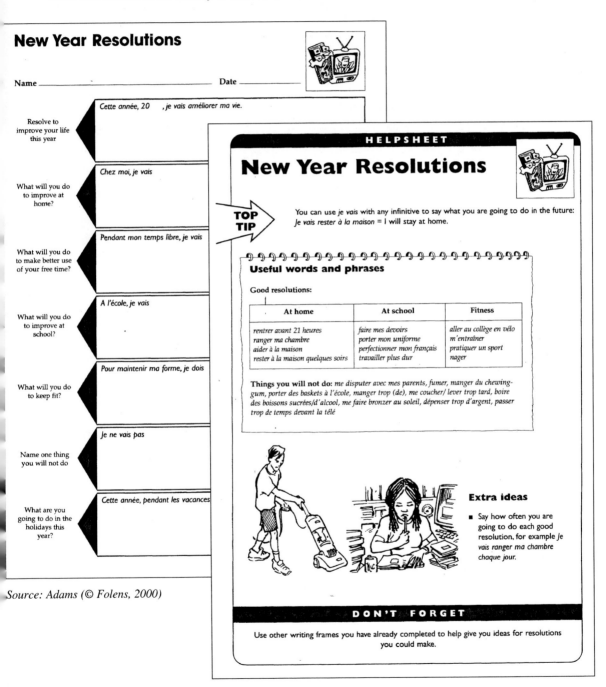

New Year Resolutions

Name _____ Date _____

Cette année, 20   , je vais améliorer ma vie.

Resolve to improve your life this year

Chez moi, je vais

What will you do to improve at home?

Pendant mon temps libre, je vais

What will you do to make better use of your free time?

A l'école, je vais

What will you do to improve at school?

Pour maintenir ma forme, je dois

What will you do to keep fit?

Je ne vais pas

Name one thing you will not do

Cette année, pendant les vacances

What are you going to do in the holidays this year?

Source: Adams (© Folens, 2000)

HELPSHEET

New Year Resolutions

TOP TIP You can use *je vais* with any infinitive to say what you are going to do in the future: *Je vais rester à la maison* = I will stay at home.

Useful words and phrases

Good resolutions:

At home	At school	Fitness
rentrer avant 21 heures	*faire mes devoirs*	*aller au collège en vélo*
ranger ma chambre	*porter mon uniforme*	*m'entraîner*
aider à la maison	*perfectionner mon français*	*pratiquer un sport*
rester à la maison quelques soirs	*travailler plus dur*	*nager*

Things you will not do: *me disputer avec mes parents, fumer, manger du chewing-gum, porter des baskets à l'école, manger trop (de), me coucher/ lever trop tard, boire des boissons sucrées/d'alcool, me faire bronzer au soleil, dépenser trop d'argent, passer trop de temps devant la télé*

Extra ideas

- Say how often you are going to do each good resolution, for example *Je vais ranger ma chambre chaque jour.*

DON'T FORGET

Use other writing frames you have already completed to help give you ideas for resolutions you could make.

WHY USE WRITING FRAMES?

Writing frames help pupils to become 'writers' in the foreign language, rather than just labellers of pictures or copiers of text. Increasingly in the National Curriculum there has been a move towards developing explicit skills in language learning and use of language. Frames contribute towards this by developing writing skills and showing how texts are constructed. Pupils joining Year 7 will be familiar with the use of writing frames from their work in Key Stage 2 and will also encounter them in other curriculum subjects in Key Stage 3.

GAMES USING A WRITING FRAME

The structured approach to writing presented in a writing frame lends itself well to writing games and group writing activities.

Carousels 1

Make a photocopy of the blank writing frame for each group. Each group writes a section of the frame (in order), then passes it on, for the next group to complete the following box. Each group ultimately does the same amount of writing, but doing this as a game adds variety.

Carousels 2

Cut the writing frame into separate sections; each group then completes one section. Reassemble the sections afterwards to see if the complete text makes sense.

Carousels 3

Each group adds to the content of each section already completed by previous groups, e.g. the first group writes: '*Je m'appelle Madonna*'. The second group adds: '*Mon nom de famille est ...*'

Consequences

This game is much the same as Carousel 1 described above, except that the teacher writes the name of the 'subject' at the bottom of the writing frame; each group fills in one section and folds it over, securing it with a paperclip, before passing it on to next group.

Mad Libs

Prepare a text with key words missing in each box of the writing frame. Number the spaces of these words. Make a list of the missing words by grammatical category. Distribute the list to pupils and ask them to predict what the missing word might be, e.g. 1. noun; 2. adjective (do not show them the frame at this point). Once pupils have written their suggestions, reveal the writing frame, and read aloud the resulting 'gap-fill'. They will probably be bizarre, but that is the point of 'Mad Libs®'! (For more details, see any of the 'Mad Libs®' books by Roger Price and Leonard Stern, or play a game on-line by doing an Internet search for 'Mad Libs'.)

DECONSTRUCTING THE TASK

Many language teachers tend to be proficient writers themselves – at least at the level of penfriend letters! This means that we seldom have to think too hard about how we would construct a simple piece of writing such as a message or note. However, most pupils cannot write 'off the cuff' in this way (especially in a foreign language) and need help in seeing what exactly each task consists of. Unfortunately we sometimes forget exactly how difficult pupils will find a writing task and overlook the combination of different skills and content areas involved in even a 'simple' writing task. Here is an example of an apparently simple writing task, showing clearly its constituent parts.

A LETTER OF COMPLAINT

- Say what you are writing about.
- Explain exactly what the problem is.
- Describe how this makes you feel.
- Say what you want done or recommend a possible solution.

One way to teach writing using this approach is to write a sample piece with each component on a separate piece of paper, Post-It note or on an OHT. Ask pupils to sort the letter/piece of writing into a logical order. Then present another model with one component missing and ask pupils to compose the missing section. Here is a game which encourages the development of similar skills:

THE WRITE IS RIGHT!

Before the lesson, the teacher writes a text onto an overhead transparency and covers key words; the pupils must guess missing words. This is basically a gap-filling exercise, but it is useful for showing the variety of ways in which a sentence or text is built up. Alison Taylor also suggests a version of this game in which the teacher writes the first word onto the board and pupils guess each subsequent word in turn. This is particularly good for focusing on sentence formation.

ALTERNATIVE WAYS OF STRUCTURING WRITING

One way of avoiding 'the fear of the blank page' is to provide boxes for pupils to write in, also subdividing the writing into several preparatory stages.

The following worksheet was designed by Deborah Gallagher at George Orwell School, Islington for use with low-ability pupils who were in their first year of learning Spanish:

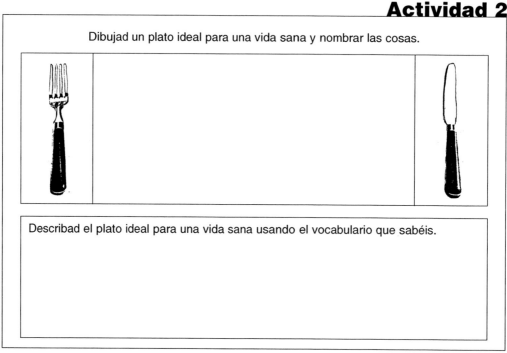

Dibujad un plato ideal para una vida sana y nombrar las cosas.

Describad el plato ideal para una vida sana usando el vocabulario que sabéis.

This very simple format helped these otherwise reluctant writers to 'get started', as the first box provided a stage which helped them to organise their ideas and collect the vocabulary they needed to use. A few pupils drew the food items, some wrote the words and some did both. This, therefore, became a way of approaching a writing task in ways suitable for different learning styles.

NEWSPAPER FORMATS

Often an attractive presentation format can make all the difference to pupils who would not otherwise write at all. We have seen the newspaper format used successfully with any number of learners of different ages and abilities. It works well for any writing task which has an initial reading stimulus, followed by a written response (See 'Using ICT for writing', p56).

USING DIALOGUE TABLES OR WRITING CHARTS

Most coursebooks include 'dialogue tables' or 'writing charts' and they are a very useful way of showing pupils how sentences are structured. The example to the right from *Zickzack neu 4* is particularly helpful in showing pupils the correct word order.

Tip des Tages

Sie sind	in die Türkei mit dem Schiff	gefahren.
Sie haben	viele Einkäufe eine Klassenfahrt	gemacht.
	ein Gymnasium mit den Schülern	besucht. getanzt.

Source: Rogers, Briggs, Goodman-Stephens and Seeger (Thomas Nelson, 1996)

CILT

However, it is often difficult to know how to use these tables creatively or for more than a simple copying task. The following two games both make effective and enjoyable use of such tables.

MASTERMIND

The teacher secretly formulates a sentence by taking one word (or phrase) from each column of the table; pupils must guess what the sentence might be and write down their suggestion. They receive points according to the number of correct words guessed. For example, using the above table:

e.g. teacher's sentence = '*Sie haben viele Einkäufe gemacht*'
Pupil 1 guesses*: Sie sind/in die Türkei/gefahren* – this gains no points
Pupil 2 guesses: **Sie haben***/ein Gymnasium/besucht* – this gains 1 point
Pupil 3 guesses: **Sie haben***/eine Klassenfahrt/***gemacht** – this gains 2 points

THE PIN GAME

In this version each item in the dialogue table is given a number (e.g. '*Sie sind*' = 1, '*Sie haben*' = 2 and so on). The teacher provides a 'PIN' (Personal Identification Number) and pupils have to construct the relevant sentence. To make this game much more challenging pupils could be required to reconstruct the sentence from memory.

This approach to dialogue tables has been used by Céline Mauris-Blanc of St Aloysius School, Islington to practise the perfect tense. The outcome was the creation of poetry which is more complex than the examples we saw in Chapter 3. Pupils have to choose carefully from the selections in each column in order to create a poem which makes sense, or to produce rhymes, e.g. *Jeudi le vent farfelu a répondu «qui es-tu?».*

Lundi	le monde	bleu	a mangé	sur la lune.
Mardi	le soleil	rouge	est allé	l'air.
Mercredi	le vent	chaud	a tué	le ciel.
Jeudi	l'oiseau	farfelu	a écouté	le nuage.
Vendredi	l'arbre	triste	a entendu	la pluie.
Samedi	le poisson	coléreux	a répondu	la femme.
Dimanche	l'homme	timide	a dit	«qui es-tu?».
		courageux	a attendu	la vie.
		impatient	a vu	la musique.
		heureux	a regardé	la terre.
		malheureux	est parti	la nature.
			a pleuré avec	dans la rivière.
				l'amour.

5. Focus on text level

To prevent pupils losing confidence and making lots of mistakes when working independently we have found it effective to give direct training to pupils to equip them to move away from the model in a gradual, controlled way. In MFL pupils need to be taken through a process of supported writing before being expected to write independently with success.

Once the teacher has enabled pupils to write a core text with the support of a model, further study of a variety of language inputs is required before the teacher can expect a variety of different outcomes from a class. Firstly, pupils need to be guided via prompts to think of content in a specified topic area that they can express using the language that they have already learnt, to change factual details in the model. (We gave an example of this in Chapter 2.)

Secondly, to train pupils to improve the style/readability of their written work the teacher can develop a 'writing surgery', sometimes also known as a 'writing workshop'. This enables pupils to write their core text first and then learn to include a list of key features whenever they compose. After the pupils have written their core text the teacher asks them to brainstorm adjectives and qualifiers and then add three to their text, for example: *assez cher … très pittoresque … trop touristique.* Next the teacher revises how to form an adverb, so that pupils can create examples using the adjectives listed earlier and everyone can add a few to their text, for example: *directement … facilement.* Now the teacher models the use of some new link words – *quand même … cependant … certes* – and pupils can suggest other familiar ones before everyone adds three to their text. The teacher can also model adding extra information using relative clauses. Pupils can work through some examples using symbols or pictures as prompts, as in the example below.

 Si vous aimez la préhistoire, allez visiter le musée où il y a beaucoup de …

Finally, pupils need to have access to additional sources of language that relate in some way to the final task. These could be listening or reading activities which focus pupils on a variety of ways of expressing the core topic sentences, an understanding of the necessary grammatical forms and useful language features.

For example, if your target assignment is a written guided tour of the town, your plan of support might include a speaking activity developing use of the polite form of the imperative. This speaking activity could be, for example, the instructions for a game. You could then introduce ideas about a town by listening to an interview of someone discussing a visit to a famous place.

CILT

For example:

- for ideas, topic sentences, e.g. 'When it comes to shopping …', 'The best place to buy your souvenirs is …', 'For a shopping trip …';

- for specialist vocabulary, e.g. medieval, urban sprawl, suburban, well restored, etc;

- study an article on career choices to provide examples of borrowable expressions – 'If you're into … then do …' or 'Do you hate mornings? Then why not become a …'.

Pupils can then decide on their own content by studying a combination of language sources or texts from different contexts with similar grammatical features. In addition they can be exposed to authentic models expressed in a different format which may provide specialist topic vocabulary and stimulate their interest.

 ## ESSAY PLANS

Once pupils are confident with a language area and how to build effective sentences, they can be supported at the 'text' level. This means that they are mainly guided with 'what' to include, rather than 'how' to say it.

The support sheet from *Mach mit! (Blatt 6.7)* on page 32 shows pupils how to structure their whole piece of writing. The assumption is made that pupils are confident with most of the language required, though they are reminded about key structures.

TRANSFER

You have learnt how to talk about the kind of television programmes you like. Now you can use that language to talk about other media.

Here are some tips
- Bring in lots of language from other units – descriptions of people and places, likes and dislikes, etc.
- Always start from the *German you already know* and not from the English you would like to translate.
- Brainstorm for expressions that will earn you bonus marks.

1 Wie heißt dein Lieblingsschauspieler / deine Lieblingsschauspielerin? Beschreib diese Person.	• You could talk about their appearance, their personality, where they live, why you like them … • This gives you lots of opportunities to show off what you know, but don't make it over-complicated (otherwise you might end up showing what you *don't* know).
2 Welche Filme magst du?	• Start with general film types, then go on to describe individual films if you want. • Take the opportunity to extend the question – say what you *don't* like and what you *prefer*.
3 Welchen Film hast du neulich gesehen? neulich = *recently* Wovon handelt er? Wer spielt die Hauptrolle?	• Don't just say the name of the film, describe it. e.g., say: – what it's about: **Er handelt von …** – who is in it: **X spielt die Hauptrolle.** – what you thought of it: **Der Film war …** • Seize the opportunity to get in a past tense (that always gets you bonus marks!): **Ich gehe nicht sehr oft ins Kino, aber letztes Jahr habe ich einen tollen Film gesehen. Er heißt …**
4 Wie viele Kinos gibt es in deiner Stadt (oder in der nächsten Stadt)? Ist es / Sind sie gut? Wo ist es / sind sie?	• You could talk about the size of building, its age, what there is next to it, opposite it, etc. You could give directions to get there (is it near a bus stop or station?). • Don't forget to give your opinion: – **Ich finde, die Kinos sind alle zu groß. Sie liegen am Stadtrand. Das ist nicht gut für das Leben in der Stadtmitte.** – **Die großen Kinos sind super. Da hat man eine gute Auswahl an Filmen und man kann auch sehr gut parken.**

Source: Berwick and Thorne (Nelson Thornes, 2001)

CILT

6. Improving writing: Teaching writers' skills

Aller Absatz ist schwer.

C'est la première page qui compte.

A text of a thousand pages begins with a single word.

We have adapted these sayings to illustrate a common problem in writing (see p80 for the original versions). Very often intermediate (and more advanced!) writers are able to write with greater ease, as long as they are helped to get started. In the journalistic context, our apprentice hack is taught very early on that most newspaper reports begin with a sentence which summarises the whole story. This is easy to illustrate using a story from an English-language newspaper – take today's newspaper and look at the first sentence of any of the news stories, and you should find a summary of the whole story in the first one or two sentences.

In the target language this also becomes a useful reading skill so that pupils know they can find a summary of the whole story in the first one or two sentences. (This technique works particularly well in German, but French newspapers mostly adopt a different style.) Journalists talk about 'answering the W questions' – where, when, why, who, what, how – to structure their writing.

A good way to practise this is to use dice from Minflashcard Games, which contain the question words. Alternatively use a normal die and provide a list of the question words for each number:

= *¿Dondé?*　　　= *¿Como?*　　　= *¿Cuando?*

If the German question words are presented in the relevant order, the dice can be useful for practising the rule of 'Time, Manner, Place' in German word order. If groups of pupils are using these dice for a writing game, when the same number/question word comes up more than once, this challenges them to expand what they have already written, e.g. if 'When?' is rolled several times:

First roll:	Yesterday
Second roll:	at 2 o'clock
Third roll:	in the afternoon
Fourth roll:	during our French lesson
Fifth roll:	after our RE lesson
Sixth roll:	before the last lesson
Seventh roll:	???

STORY STARTERS

You can also draw pupils' attention to the use of 'Once upon a time ...' and introduce them to the target-language equivalents.

You could invent similar standard formulae to help pupils get going on a piece of writing. For example, in the coursework context we have seen the following used very successfully, which as well as helping the writer to get started, also uses two tenses and an opinion in the very first sentence: *Je vais écrire au sujet de ..., parce que ...*

It is easy to find examples of ways in which such writing is structured in the 'real world'. These can be shared with pupils to illustrate good practice in learning to write. Where these are used in the target language they can also be useful reading strategies. A more complex version for advanced writers would be to use rhetorical questions, e.g. What would school be like without teachers?

LINK WORDS: *ET!* – EH?

When pupils learn to read in English, 'and' is one of the twelve most common words they encounter. The following words are among the 100 most common words, which comprise a half of all reading material:

as	*but*	*first*	*now*	*or*
so	*then*	*when*	*which*	*with*

(Adapted from Whitrod 1982: 11)

Unfortunately, when learning a foreign language, pupils often lack these basic building blocks so are unable to produce anything but the most simple, contracted, repetitive sentences. Such language is unlikely to make them feel a sense of achievement in their writing. Similarly, one of the elements of writing which raises attainment beyond the level of a Grade C at GCSE level, is that pupils write cohesive text which is not overly disjointed in structure. Such small words are not learnt 'by osmosis', but they are easy to overlook when focusing on teaching nouns, verbs and adjectives illustrated on flashcards. Here are some ideas for including link words in your teaching.

AND	connects two related ideas. When you are drilling new language, include two items in whatever word or structure the pupils are practising: *Je voudrais un coca ET un Orangina.* *Je joue au foot ET au tennis.*
BUT	connects two contrasting ideas. Provide a list of adjectives in contrasting groups and ask pupils to select one adjective from each group for their description: *Ma maison est petite MAIS moderne.* *Mon ami est intelligent MAIS farfelu.*
OR	links alternatives. Ask pupils to choose two answers each time: *Je voudrais devenir astronaute OU neurochirurgien.* *Mes feuilletons préférés sont EastEnders OU The Archers.*
BECAUSE	links an outcome with its explanation. Ask pupils to create plausible (or silly!) explanations from lists: *Je n'ai pas fait mes devoirs PARCE QU'il y avait un orage.* *Je veux aller en ville PARCE QU'il y a un bon film.*
SO	links cause and effect. Use the same language as above in the opposite order: *Il y avait un orage DONC je n'ai pas fait mes devoirs.* *Il y a un bon film DONC je veux aller en ville.*
SEQUENCE WORDS	show what order something has occurred in. Ask pupils to describe their school uniform, but describing in what order they put on the items of clothing: *D'ABORD je mets ma chemise, ET PUIS je mets mon pantalon ...* *FINALEMENT je mets mon chapeau.*

These ideas provide starting points for the use of link words, but more sophisticated items can be added when pupils are ready. The link words used, and the stage at which they are introduced will vary in different languages, but it is usually best to start with those words most familiar to pupils in English, such as 'and', 'but', 'then', 'because'. Other possible teaching points include:

- for example;
- perhaps;
- also;
- supposing;
- despite;
- consequently;
- if/whether;
- neither/nor;
- not only/but also;
- whilst;
- on the other hand;
- in order to;
- a wider range of time phrases and sequence words.

Once pupils are confident with a range of link words, they can use them to improve pieces of writing by editing with link words, in exercises designed specifically for this purpose. In feedback, make it clear that there is often more than one suitable word. Here is a sample activity to practise link words in German (answers on p80):

Choose from:
aber | also | auch | dann | nur | oder | um ... zu | und | vielleicht | weil | zuerst

Ich heiße Carl ...**(1)**... wohne in Swindon in Südengland. Ich bin Einzelkind, ...**(2)**... ich habe viele Kusinen, die alle in Swindon wohnen. Ich gehe noch zur Schule, ...**(3)**... nächstes Jahr möchte ich Fremdsprachen studieren. Mein Lieblingsfach ist Französisch, ...**(4)**... weil ich in Kanada gewohnt habe. ...**(5)**... habe ich in Irland gewohnt, aber ...**(6)**... sind wir nach Kanada gezogen. Ich finde Geschichte ganz einfach, ...**(7)**... es sehr interessant ist. Ich möchte später ...**(8)**... Spanisch lernen. Ich möchte nächstes Jahr nach Deutschland fahren, ...**(9a)**... mein Deutsch ...**(9b)**... verbessern. Das kostet viel Geld, ...**(10)**... bisher habe ich ...**(11)**... ganz wenig Geld gespart!

CiLT

We have found the *Key to GCSE French writing skills* by Crossland and Horsfall (1998) useful for developing such 'writers' skills'. Each sheet covers a range of ways in which pupils can improve their writing and provides a practice text for pupils to apply the skills just taught. In this exercise pupils are being shown how to improve the style and content of their writing in a variety of ways.

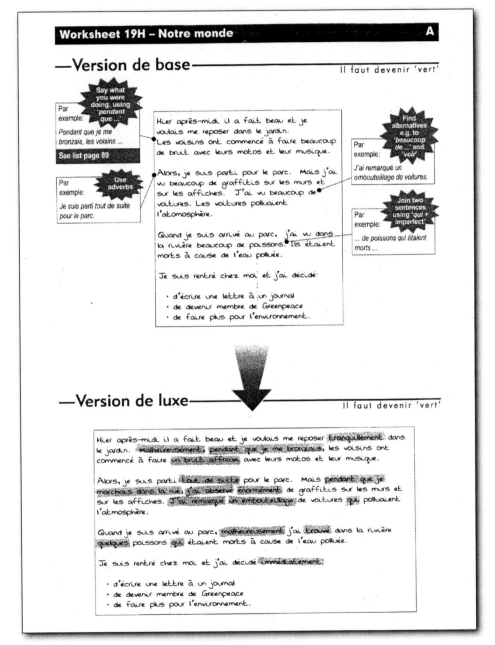

Source: Crossland and Horsfall (John Murray, 1998)

DRAFTING AND EDITING

Creative writing often suffers because children are not given sufficient opportunities for redrafting their work, after constructive criticisms from their teacher and from other pupils. It is not surprising that redrafting happens less often than it should. The time and effort involved in the physical act of writing is a considerable barrier for young children to overcome. (Schenk 1986: 42)

Teaching pupils to edit their own writing involves more than asking them to 'copy out their work in best'. 'Copying up' implies only improving the presentation, so has little merit educationally. In fact, sometimes pupils' work deteriorates the more they are asked to 'copy up'! We need to aim for drafting and editing to become a regular part of the routine of writing. Our colleagues in the English department often spend a large part of their capitation on 'drafting books', so that pupils retain all the drafts of their work in one place. This helps to show pupils that it is possible to improve their writing, rather than being content with the first attempt. Drafting and editing are also an important part of a 'portfolio' approach to writing. As so much of our subject is 'ephemeral' (for example, a 30-second speaking activity with no physical outcome or evidence), building up portfolios of written work is a good way for pupils to have tangible evidence of the progress they are making.

However, pupils need to be taught how to edit their own work, as few will do it naturally. Strategies to reinforce editing skills that can be effective are:

- A pupil reads his/her work out, the teacher questions the class, asking for 'advice' and a correct version is written on the OHP or board by the teacher or a pupil. Key points can then be drawn from this to create a checklist before pupils follow the editing process individually.

- Pupils read their work out loud in pairs and, using reference materials, collaborate to correct each other's work.

- The teacher guides the editing process by taking in the transcripts and identifying the most common errors which are then discussed with examples with the whole class before individual pupils edit their own work.

- 'Lucky dip'. This is a game which gives pupils a reason for careful proof-reading and a context for editing. Everyone writes 'on behalf of' another person in the same class; afterwards the 'victim' edits the text together with the author, for example instead of writing about your own holiday you write about your victim's.

- Display a list of drafting conventions on the classroom wall, just as you might for classroom language or markschemes and so on. It is then more likely that pupils will see that drafting and editing are an expected process of writing, rather than just being told when they get things 'wrong'.

A checklist for correct writing (in French) might include some of the items below. (These lists are quite extensive, which some pupils might find off-putting. Initially you might focus on two or three times from each list.) A checklist for German would include different items, such as **Capital Letters on all Nouns.**

CILT

Checking your writing	Improving your writing
☐ Have you checked the gender? Do you need *le* or *la,* or *un* or *une?*	☐ Is your text in a logical order?
☐ Are you describing an item which is feminine? If so, have you checked the endings on the adjectives?	☐ Have you included detailed descriptions?
	☐ Have you used more than one tense?
☐ Are you using the perfect tense? If so, have you used the right past participle? Have you got the right part of *être* or *avoir?*	☐ Have you used opinions?
	☐ Have you repeated any word or phrase too much?
☐ Are there any spellings you're not sure of?	☐ Have you joined sentences wherever possible?
☐ Do you have the right word for 'he/she' or 'his/her'?	☐ Have you described the 'action' with adverbs?
☐ Have you got the right ending on all the verbs?	
☐ Have you checked the punctuation?	
☐ If you have made any alterations, are they clear?	**checklist**
☐ Have you checked your facts?	

The following game can be helpful in developing appropriate editing skills. It requires learners to focus on the accuracy of their writing if they are to win the game.

WHISPER WHISPER

This can be played in groups and is particularly good for practising messages. The teacher starts the game by whispering a sentence to the first pupil in each line. The pupil at end of each line must write down the whispered sentence. Then the whole class compares the whispered versions with the teacher's original, which is good for focusing on accuracy.

 ## EXTENDING WRITING

Many pupils reach a stage at which their writing is simple and accurate, but very repetitive, using the same core words all the time. It can be quite easy to teach pupils to broaden the content of their writing by offering them lists of alternatives to key phrases, and very often these 'more difficult' or 'more impressive' words are cognates. You could also use the approaches suggested in earlier chapters, where the teacher presents a very 'bland' piece of writing and pupils are invited to make it as expressive as possible. The following list in English gives ideas on areas to develop in the target language, with suggestions for alternatives:

- to go = visit, explore, *se rendre à*
- to say = declare, exclaim, reply, shout, cry, report, insist
- much/many/very = so much, loads of, various, numerous
- good = fabulous, world-beating, unbelievable
- bad = terrible, shocking, boring
- there is/there are = we have/one has, is situated (e.g. *se trouver, sich befinden*)

7. Creativity in writing

In this chapter we look at a variety of ideas which allow learners to exploit relatively modest amounts of the foreign language in a creative way. One potential problem of open-ended creative tasks is that pupils might want to write a complicated plot and falter on their lack of language. On the other hand, some learners are intimidated by open-ended tasks and never even start to write. Therefore, this is yet another area of writing where we need to guide and support possible responses. For the first type of learner described above, this may restrict what they actually want to write, but will help them to produce an outcome with an acceptable level of accuracy. The other type of learner will be supported by this approach and should be able to start writing.

GETTING CREATIVE

We have given examples of creative tasks throughout this book, which require only small amounts of language to produce an attractive outcome (see for example, pp13 and 17–18), but here are a few more tasks we have found successful. Creative writing need not involve large amounts of words. Often an impressive effect can be achieved by putting together several smaller pieces of writing.

THE BIRTHDAY-CARD TASK

Nominate someone celebrating their birthday – this can be a real, fictional or an imaginary character. Ask pupils to write birthday cards from as many people as they can think. For example, for the Queen's birthday, she could receive cards from: her husband, her children, her grandchildren, her corgis, the Prime Minister, a loyal subject, foreign royalty, the soldier who stands outside her palace … This is a good way of practising family vocabulary and names of jobs. This task can be done individually or collectively.

Die Arbeitskollegen bei der Firma **AMS Finanz** gratulieren Frau Dr. Gertrud Malinowski zum 50. Geburtstag

Ein Dicker Kuß von Deinem Enkelkind Tim

ICH BIN NOCH KEINE 50 TAGE ALT ABER ICH LIEBE DICH!

Liebe Mutti! Ein halbes Jahrhundert ist nicht so viel! Karl und Johanna

CILT

FLIP-FLAP BOOKS OR 'PHOTO-ROBOT'

Ask each pupil to write a brief description of a person's face and draw a picture to illustrate it on a piece of paper, as shown below. Compile the pictures and descriptions and then cut each description along the relevant horizontal lines (this could, of course, be done by a pupil). These books are also known as 'mix and match' books and most young learners will be familiar with them from children's books. It is our experience that pupils often volunteer to write more than one description in this activity! This also works with, for example, descriptions of a house. The book could also be themed, for example, 'flip-flaps' of The Spice Girls, characters in the Big Brother house, and need not be restricted to physical descriptions.

DIAMOND 9

If you use 'Diamond 9' or other prioritising activities, wherever possible ask the pupils to write or decide on the items they will later be prioritising. In this 'Diamond 9' task the class is divided into nine groups and each has to write a simple menu. These are then used for a sorting activity where pupils decide on the relative nutritional value of each menu.

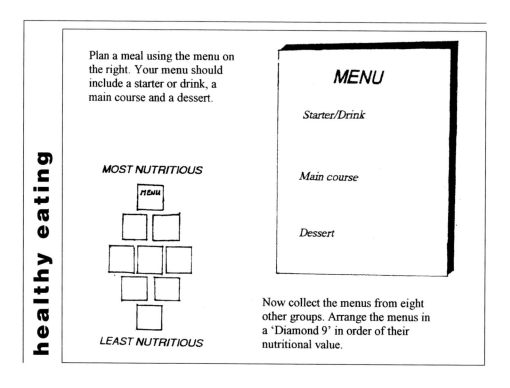

Plan a meal using the menu on the right. Your menu should include a starter or drink, a main course and a dessert.

healthy eating

MOST NUTRITIOUS

MENU

LEAST NUTRITIOUS

MENU

Starter/Drink

Main course

Dessert

Now collect the menus from eight other groups. Arrange the menus in a 'Diamond 9' in order of their nutritional value.

EXPANDING CREATIVITY AND CITIZENSHIP

Creativity in writing is not just about stories and poems, but also about expanding pupils' experience of the world – in other words all the requirements of section 4 of the NC Programme of Study 'Developing cultural awareness'. MFL teachers have a key role to play in widening pupils' cultural knowledge and understanding in the new citizenship curriculum. With the correct materials and support it is possible to cover intercultural topics in a way which is interesting and non-threatening.

The task opposite is taken from the ALL *French writing activities for KS4* and prepares learners for a writing activity about the position and role of children in different countries. Pupils start with a reading task about families in Algeria, then they interview each other. The questions then provide the necessary structure for writing up the results of one of the interviews.

CiLT

Les enfants

2 Combien de nationalités différentes sont représentées dans ton école?

a   Interroge trois personnes (ou plus) d'une nationalité différente de la tienne.
Pose ces questions (utilise un dictionnaire si nécessaire).

b   Ecris les réponses dans un tableau:

nom	né(e) à/ en/au	nationalité	position des filles*	position des garçons*
Tejinder	Karachi, Pakistan	Pakistanaise	en général inférieure	en général supérieure
			* supérieure/inférieur/égale	

1 Tu es né(e) en Grande-Bretagne?
2 Ta famille vient d'où?
3 Est-ce que dans ce pays,
• les garçons sont plus importants que les filles?
• les filles sont plus importantes que les garçons?
• la position des filles et des garçons est égale?

3 Choisis le plus intéressant de tes interviews. Ecris-le au propre.

Source: ALL French writing activities for KS4 *by Swarbrick, Calvert and Gordon (© ALL, 1997)*

The writing frame below (which links with Unit 5 of the QCA KS3 Schemes of Work) supports pupils in writing about their own school life while comparing it with another culture.

Comparing schools

Name ————————————————————— Date ——————————

Introduce yourself and your school briefly – which town and country is your school in?	Je suis élève au collège C'est à en / au
Which days do you go to school? And in the other country?	Nous allons à l'école Mais en / au / aux / à la / à l' on va à l'école
What time do you start school? And in the other country?	Nous commençons à heures. Mais en / au / aux / à la / à l' on commence à heures.
Which subjects do you study? And in the other country?	Nous étudions Mais en / au / aux / à la / à l' on étudie
At what age did you start French? And when do they start English in the other country?	Nous commençons le français à l'âge de Mais en / au / aux / à la / à l' on commence l'anglais à l'âge de
What and where do you eat at lunch-time? And in the other country?	A midi, nous mangeons Mais en / au / aux / à la / à l' on mange
What sports do you do at school? And in the other country?	Nous faisons du sport à l'école, par exemple Mais en / au / aux / à la / à l' on
Which country would you prefer to go to school in? Why?	Je préférerais être élève en / au / aux / à la / à l' parce que

Source: French writing frames: Creative and imaginative writing by Adams (© Folens, 2000)

CiLT

The activity below is taken from *Creative Key Stage 4 French* and is part of a writing game in which pupils reconstruct a description of a typical day of a Haitian boy. This means that pupils are simultaneously practising their memory and writing skills and rehearsing the language of the personal identification and daily routine topics, while increasing their knowledge and understanding of life in another context.

Une journée à Haïti

Je m'appelle Riclaude Datte, et j'ai 19 ans. J'habite à Côtes de Fer avec mes parents et mes six frères et soeurs. Voici une journée typique de ma vie.

A six heures du matin _____ _____. Puis je me lave et _____. Normalement _____ _____; Souvent, _____ assez à manger à la maison.	A treize heures, _____ devoirs, je travaille dans les jardins et _____ _____ _____ alors il faut cultiver _____.	_____ je me couche. Je suis _____ _____.
L'école finit à _____, et je rentre _____. Chaque jour_____, mais _____ je ne les fais pas _____.	_____, nous dînons. Normalement _____ _____ ce sont des spaghettis avec des carottes. _____ et _____ _____il faut prendre soin des animaux.	Je quitte la maison _____ _____ Je vais à l'école à pied – _____ _____. Quelques-uns de mes amis doivent marcher _____ _____ pour aller à l'école.
_____, à seize heures _____ _____. Si mon ami est _____ pour ses parents, je l'aide. Mes amis font _____la même chose pour moi.	A huit heures du matin ____ _____ Mon école s'appelle l'École _____. Je suis dans la dernière classe _____ _____ _____: les maths, le français, les sciences.	_____ est à dix heures. _____ _____ tout le monde cherche des fruits pour manger: _____ _____ _____il y a des arbres fruitiers près de l'école.

The source material for *La Journée de Riclaude Datte* is reproduced by kind permission of ActionAid

Source: Raithby and Taylor (© MLG Publishing, 2001)

STORY WRITING

Because narrative is closer to speech, children usually find this kind of writing easier than description, argument and other kinds of non-narrative writing which are organised rather differently. (Edwards 1995: 15)

Story telling is something that comes naturally to young children and yet adolescent learners of a foreign language find it very difficult. This is often because the sophistication of their story outreaches the language they have at their disposal. However, story telling can be made accessible if appropriate support for structure and vocabulary is provided.

It is clear that stories can motivate learners very effectively in learning the target language. It is not uncommon for people who learned a foreign language using the Nuffield *Forwards* series to be able to recite large parts of the stories, or to make pilgrimages to Cadolzburg to meet the real-live Hans and Liselotte! The power of story telling is now used in some accelerated learning language courses where units of work are based on the stories of the characters in the book. This means that pupils come to associate particular language points with characters.

It is possible to support story writing while still permitting pupils to choose much of the content or the settings. *Lernpunkt Deutsch 1* contains a useful idea with much support for weak writers. In the exercise opposite, pupils just have to select one answer from three possibilities to create their desired story from the flowchart. Arguably, pupils are engaged in a higher level of reading than writing in this task, but they still have their own version of the story as a written outcome and are learning how to construct stories.

The grid pictured on page 48 from *Encouraging writing* builds on the above idea, turning the choice of story setting, character and context into a dice game (Tainsh 1991: 48). This could easily be adapted to suit foreign language topics. For example, instead of the traditional children's story contexts, pupils could be offered a choice between school, at the café, at the leisure centre and so on.

👤 Tagesablauf

1 Schreib deinen Tagesablauf auf. Du hast die Wahl ...

a Du bist ein ganz normaler Schüler/eine ganz normale Schülerin.
b Du bist ein Vampir.
c Du bist ein Schüler oder eine Schülerin im Jahr 2058.

Mit Hilfe eines Wörterbuchs, wähl die passenden Wörter unten und schreib die Geschichte auf.

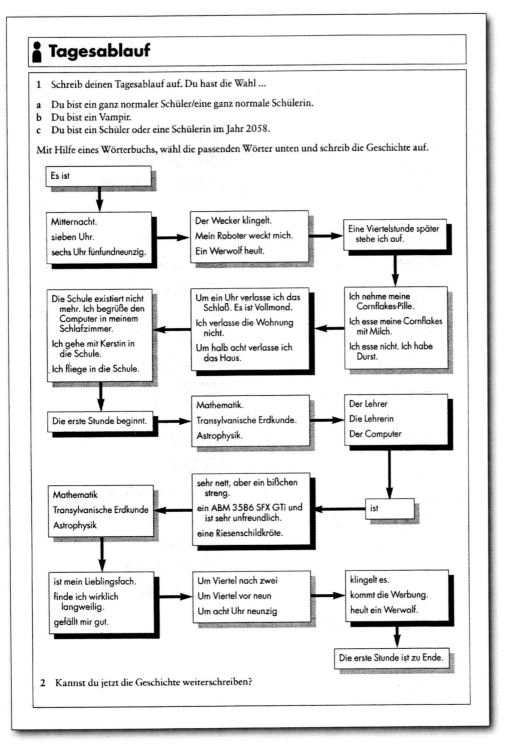

2 Kannst du jetzt die Geschichte weiterschreiben?

Source: Morris and Wesson (© Thomas Nelson, 1996)

THE STORY GAME CHART

A TYPE OF STORY		B SETTING	C CHARACTERS	D EVENTS	E ENDING?
1. HORROR		Town. House. Castle	Dracula. Animals. Vampires. Ghosts	Death. Chases	**?**
2. SCIENCE FICTION		Space. Lab. Underwater.	Astronaut. Diver. Professor.	Travel. Flights. Experiments.	**?**
3. ROMANCE		School. Offices. Disco. Party. Hospital.	Man. Woman. Boy. Girl. Teacher. Friend. Filmstar. Doctor	Parties. Break-ups. Dates. Discos. Weddings.	**?**
4. ADVENTURE		Desert. Forest. Temples. Jungle. Sea. Tombs. Lost cities.	Hero. Heroine. Baddies. Villains. Ghosts.	Murders. Chases. Discoveries. Escapes. Captures.	**?**
5. FAIRY		Castle. Garden. Cave	Princess. Prince. Fairy Godmother. Elves. Witches.	Spells. Kidnaps. Deaths.	**?**
6. WESTERN		Desert. Ranch. Frontier town. Saloon bar. Barber's shop. Jail.	Baddies. Cowboys. indians. Sheriff	Chases. Break-outs. Gunfights. Duels. Death.	**?**

Source: Tainsh (© Folens, 1991)

SOAP AND GOSSIP

Pupils are genuinely interested in the stories they hear and see in soap operas. One way to build their confidence in story writing is therefore through re-telling the stories of soap operas. Provide them with key phrases such as:

> *... s'est disputé(e) avec ...*   *... a volé ...*   *... est tombé(e) amoureux/se de ...*
> *... est mort(e)*   *Il/elle a dit ...*

Pupils are also motivated by gossip and see plenty of models of this kind of writing in magazines and newspapers. A 'gossip column' activity can be based on a particular event such as the Oscars, the Brit Awards or even just a normal week's soap viewing. Key phrases in this area include:

> *On l'a vu(e) avec ...*   *Il/elle sort avec ...*   *Il/elle a cassé avec ...*
> *Il/elle achète ses vêtements chez ...*   *et il/elle porte ...*

CILT

BRANCHING STORIES

Branching stories might appeal to those (particularly boys) who play 'Dungeons and dragons' type games. Again, several people or groups can contribute small amounts of writing to build up into a larger story. You might find it difficult to write such stories yourself and follow each branch of the story through to its logical conclusion, but learners who play such games will find it straightforward. The key factor in branching stories is that the reader must be presented with a decision at the end of each section This format can also be used to write stories within the context of the usual transactional topics, such as planning a trip to the target language country. For example, you ask for two airline tickets but are told the price has increased. Do you still go by plane? Yes – go to ... No – go to ... One easy way to arrange such stories is on cards, with each 'page' on a separate card. It also works well in word-processing with hyperlinks.

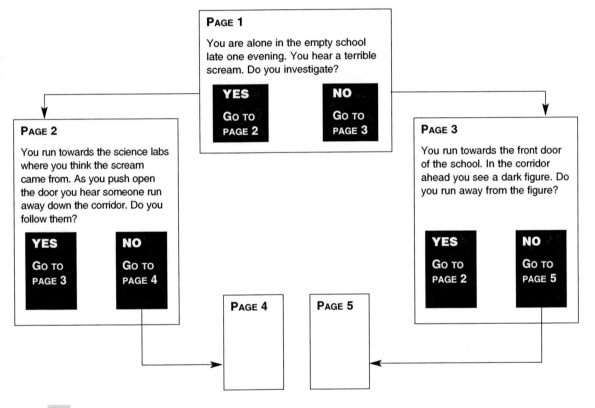

DREAMS

Dreams are a useful context for getting learners to write creatively, as they provide the opportunity to use the past tense and write lots of descriptions. Learners can also be supported in using lots of temporal connectives such as 'firstly, then, suddenly ...'. Writing about dreams is often used in creative writing workshops for adults as it allows inexperienced writers to draw on ideas from their unconscious.

8. Letter writing

In the research for *The invisible child* (Lee *et al* 1998) pupils were asked, 'What is the best thing you have achieved in your (French/German) work so far?'. Their answers included a 'heavy emphasis on productive skills' and they named tasks such as: 'writing a letter that could be sent abroad … writing a practice letter well … writing independently a long letter to a penfriend, learning to write longer passages' (*ibid:* 33). Indeed, we all use the ubiquitous task of 'Write a letter to your penfriend about …' and it is the standard fare of the GCSE terminal writing paper. Unfortunately this means that letter-writing tasks can become overused in the MFL classroom and are greeted with reactions such as:

- 'We've done this before.'
- 'But I haven't got a penfriend.'
- 'No one's going to read it anyway.'
- 'If I wanted to tell one of my friends something, I'd phone them up!'

In Chapter 10 we talk about the importance of an audience for writing. Letters seem to have an 'automatic' audience, but unless they are sent to this audience, this aspect of motivation can fall flat, or even be counterproductive. Ann Clark thinks that boys have a particular problem with letter writing as letters, notes and invitations are 'more likely to appeal to girls and the ways in which they have been socialised' (Clark 1998: 31). (Moreover boys tend to dislike writing about themselves.) The first point to make about using letter writing as a task is not to overuse it, especially with boys. There are many writing tasks which make sense without putting them into the context of a letter. For example, instead of asking pupils to write a letter to their (non-existent) penfriend about their favourite subjects at school, ask pupils to write an account of their progress at school, similar to the kind of profile they would write (in English) for their Record of Achievement.

MAKING LETTER WRITING MEANINGFUL

Concetta Maida of Islington Green School produced a very motivating unit of work for Year 7 Italian pupils based on an exchange of letters with (imaginary) Italian pupils. First of all, the English pupils read letters from Italian pupils introducing themselves. They then selected one letter and wrote a reply, telling their correspondent all about themselves. This included almost all of the materials they had covered during Year 7. Rather than 'marking' their work, Concetta instead used her time to write short replies to each pupil which covered any language points the pupils had got wrong in their own letter. At the end of this unit of work the pupils also had the opportunity to fill in a (real) application form for a penfriend society.

Post offices often run campaigns to encourage letter writing among young people. The Deutsche Post AG runs 'LetterNet', a particularly attractive scheme which gives each respondent a free writing set and address book (LetterNet, Postfach 100 100, D-12701, Berlin, Germany).

PLAN INTERNATIONAL

Plan International is a child-sponsoring agency which involves the UK-based sponsor corresponding with a child in a developing country. This correspondence includes letters to and from the child, and every year a set of photos of the child and family members is sent to the sponsor. These letters are usually in the country's official language with a translation into English. It is possible for school groups to sponsor a child and it is also possible to request to sponsor a boy or girl, or a child in a particular country, including many Francophone and Hispanic countries. Plan International supplies suggested formats for letters and cards which are mainly to support younger children in writing to their 'foster-cousin'. Adapting these to the target language could prove a worthwhile task for KS3/4 pupils. It is also a cause of genuine interest when a letter arrives from the child. Plan International provides regular information about the community in which the sponsored child lives, and this could form the basis for some very worthwhile learning about the target-language speaking country.

Plan International UK, 5–6 Underhill Street, London NW1 7HS.
Tel: 020 7485 6612
www.plan-international.org.uk

Julie Adams's Senegalese foster child, Moussou, with her brother Boubacal

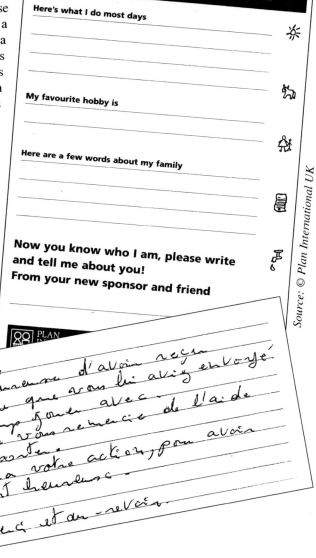

POSTCARDS AND NOTES

Instead of postcards and notes, try placing shorter 'message' tasks in the context of mobile phone 'text messaging'. Pupils need to understand that a foreign correspondent would not understand the conventions and abbreviations used in English. However, the challenge to write the message as briefly as possible while still retaining the full sense would be motivating to some. In fact, a useful guided writing task could be to adapt the teacher's message into one which would take the fewest number of keystrokes whilst still transmitting the full content. If pupils are required to cover a list of content points, this can be a good way to revise meeting the list of criteria in GCSE terminal paper writing tasks.

Postcard and short letter-writing tasks can be made more motivating by allowing pupils to write on free advertising postcards. Racks of these postcards are often found in cafés and cinemas. The completed postcards then lend themselves to a colourful display.

THE JOLLY POSTMAN

For children – and teachers – who are fans of *The jolly postman*, it is worth buying a copy of *Pen pals: A friendship in French and English* (Bruzzone and Morton 1998), which contains real letters, envelopes, a map and a mini phrase book. It is apparently aimed at the KS2 market, and although one of the main characters is a boy, it probably contains too many hearts and butterflies to capture the interest of most KS3 boys. However, the idea is still very engaging and can be used in the classroom for reading for pleasure and as a model from which pupils can write their own correspondence. Pupils can make their own books out of sugar paper (see book-making idea on p63) and create their own letters, postcards, maps, guides, phrase books, etc to insert. Working in pairs/small groups would give pupils the opportunity to centre the correspondence on their own interests: football fans could describe and/or invent the various successes of the teams of the English and French correspondent respectively.

If you were doing this project in Russian, writing the envelopes would be of particular value as the layout is different from that usually used in Western Europe.

USING ICT IN LETTER WRITING

There is a tendency to think that letters are more appropriately written by hand, but one context where word-processing fits in particularly well with letter writing is writing 'mystery' letters, where the object is to disguise the handwriting. Pupils each word-process a letter about themselves and their interests/favourite subjects, etc but omitting their name. These letters are printed out and displayed with a number. This display can now be used in two ways. Either pupils try to guess the identity of each letter-writer, or pupils from another class can select a suitable correspondent and write a reply. The latter task also fits in well with the 'Lonely hearts' context.

A similar task is to ask pupils to write to another person making a request, e.g. to a grandparent asking for a new computer, to the local MP asking for a new sports centre to be built, to the headteacher asking for a reduction in the amount of homework. Pupils then read each other's (anonymous) letters and decide whether the request should be granted, also writing a short justification of their decisions. Such ideas can fit in well with 'active citizenship' campaigns.

Formal letters also lend themselves well to being word-processed, for example, a standard letter for booking a pitch at a campsite. In this case, the teacher prepares a standard letter, which pupils then alter on-screen for their own reservations. As support, pupils could have a gap-fill letter with the necessary information given as symbols (these symbols would be the same as those used at the presentation stage).

Pupils could also be encouraged to produce their own pro-forma letters which require only personal details and so on to be filled in. Pupils will have seen such proforma letters used at school and this task will help to illustrate that they can learn a standard format in the target language to adapt as necessary.

 E-MAIL PROJECTS

E-mail is obviously advantageous for providing a realistic context for writing letters and messages. Help with setting up e-mail links with schools abroad can be obtained from:

www.epals.com	www.europict.org	www.gconn.co.uk

The main advice in setting up e-mails as a classroom task is to write on a specific topic for a given length of time, e.g. pupils have to survey their target language counterparts about hobbies, favourite school subjects, etc. Such topics can also work well if pupils are paired with another pupil in the same country. E-mail is also an important feature of 'tandem learning' which is one-to-one communication between two native speakers of different languages, who are each learners of the other's language. You can read more details about the Tandem Learning Project on: www.slf.ruhr-uni-bochum.de/email/idxeng00.html. For a full report of the two-year Lingua-D *Tandem Schule* project read *Tandem language learning in schools* (Gläsmann and Calvert, 2000).

9. Using ICT for writing

There is not the room in this chapter to cover all of the issues involved in using ICT in the MFL classroom, or to give very precise instructions of how this should be done. Instead, this chapter gives an introduction to some of the ideas involved in using ICT to encourage children to write in the foreign language, as well as some practical ideas.

ADVANTAGES AND DISADVANTAGES OF USING ICT

+	**–**
• Children tend to be motivated by ICT.	• 'Typing up' work previously written elsewhere is not a productive use of either MFL contact time or computer time.
• Work produced in a virtual format can easily be edited and redrafted.	
• Written work can be transmitted via various communications media.	• Using ICT can detract from quality of the written work, e.g. by devoting too much time to fancy formats and inserting pictures.
• Written work can be published in attractive formats.	
• Using clipart or pictures downloaded from the Internet means that pupils can devote their time to writing rather than drawing.	• Many learners are far less accurate when using ICT than when writing by hand.
	• It can be difficult to find foreign accents, thus discouraging their use.

On balance, the advantages of ICT use can outweigh any drawbacks, and of course we are statutorily required to use ICT in delivering our subject. Below we include several tried and tested ideas for using ICT in the MFL classroom, divided according to the type of software or application.

WRITING IDEAS FOR WORD-PROCESSING

Word-processing provides two main opportunities for use in the MFL classroom: writing your own text or sorting other people's text using 'drag and drop' facilities. Either of these can provide good opportunities for re-drafting and editing. It is important to provide opportunities to become confident in word-processing, as this forms the basis of so many other applications such as e-mail, web publishing and presentation packages such as PowerPoint.

'DRAG AND DROP' TASKS

- Sort a jumbled dialogue into the correct order using 'copy, cut and paste' or 'highlight and drag'. Ensure that each new line of dialogue is on a separate line. It is also possible to do this as a game on *Fun with texts* (see p59).

- Find a rhyming poem in the TL. Write each line of the poem on a new line on-screen and jumble up the order. Pupils have to use their knowledge of the link between pronunciation and writing to rearrange the poem into a possible order. (*Fun with texts* does this automatically.)

- Provide a map or picture on-screen – pupils have to read the description in order to drag and drop the labels into the correct place. A more difficult version of this idea would be to provide pupils with a correctly labelled picture or map, which pupils then have to use to correct a written description.

- Use a table in Word to create a picture of a house. Write the names of the rooms beneath. Pupils then use 'drag and drop' to label the house correctly. This idea also works with town plans, descriptions of layout of bedroom, etc.

- Provide a list of days of the week or months which pupils have to sort into the correct order.

- To practise the written form of numbers, provide a set of number words which learners have to sort into the given numeral, for example > > >

- In the topic of celebrations, pupils use 'drag and drop' to sort a list of vocabulary they have encountered during the presentation stage: *des fleurs, du champagne, des cartes, la cheminée, à la mosquée …*

On mange	On offre	On allume	On écrit	On boit	On va	On chante

Pupils then use this vocabulary support to write simple sentences about each festival, e.g. *Pour célébrer Hanoukka, on allume des bougies.*

CREATING TEXT

- Pupils are given a description on-screen and have to compare it to a picture; they then correct the mistakes in the written description. As an extension task, they could improve the description by adding more detail.

- Provide a picture of a suspect for which pupils have to write a 'Wanted' poster. As an extension task, pupils also write sentences in the past tense describing what the suspect did.

- Write a dialogue and delete occasional lines. Pupils invent their own responses to the gaps and then perform their role-play to the rest of the class.

- Design a form to make a reservation at a tourist office, for example, for a trip or journey, accommodation, or to go to an event.

- A carousel writing activity – divide the class into groups. The first group writes a few lines describing a holiday they have just heard about on tape (or prompt this with pictures). The groups then move to a different computer and now work on a piece of writing started by another group. Each subsequent group adds to the description, so the activity gets harder as it goes along. If you are doing this activity with one computer as part of a carousel, allow the least able group of writers to go first and the most able to go last (when it is harder to think of something else to write which hasn't already been written).

- Use the newspaper format to present reading and writing exercises – the first column contains the source text and pupils write/draw their response in the right-hand column. This newspaper format is quite easy to do in Microsoft Word (switch to View/Page Layout; Format/Columns). Alternatively use Tables to present text in columns.

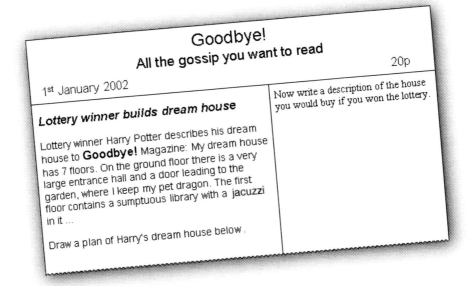

WRITING IDEAS FOR E-MAIL

- For a short-term e-mail project, pair pupils with a class in another school (either here or in the target-language country). They are given the task of finding out about each other using e-mail. It helps if pupils draft their messages in advance before being allowed to enter e-mail. Pupils ask specific questions about, for example, the timetable at partner's school, or survey questions.

- Pair reluctant writers with a native speaker, foreign language assistant or older pupil. The native speaker corrects their correspondent's messages and sends back a re-drafted version of the text. Sometimes their response might include an explanation of a grammar or spelling point.

WRITING IDEAS FOR THE INTERNET

- Ask pupils to analyse web pages (nominated by the teacher) using a list of criteria (clarity of text, interest of content, usefulness of pictures, etc). After drafting, pupils then use the web-page template on Word to create their own individual web page describing themselves, a teacher or a famous person. Pupils can also bring their own pictures and photos to scan into the page. The page contains text which is presented in various fonts and pupils should be restricted to just two pictures per page (to ensure they spend more time writing in the TL rather than manipulating pictures). Only those pupils who have completed previous homework (draft design and text for web page) are permitted to start this activity. When completed, pupils could load their web page onto the school website, print it out for their portfolio or put it onto disk and send it to their partner school (see Chapter 10 for publishing ideas).

- In a unit of work on lost property (in Spanish), pupils visit **www.objetosperditos.com** and submit a report about a lost article. This is a real website and should the article be 'found' the pupil would receive an e-mail telling them (although this is unlikely, especially if they describe wacky items!).

- Use on-line postcard facilities to send an electronic postcard to the teacher or other nominated person. For example, the visitor site **www.hamburg.de** has on-line postcards.

- Use electronic greeting cards in the target language including a short text – pupils could send these to a nominated person, or send to themselves to print out. The greeting-cards website **www.bluemountain.com** has a large range of cards in various languages.

WRITING IDEAS FOR POWERPOINT

- PowerPoint is useful for providing multi-sensory learning opportunities, as it can integrate sound, text, pictures and movement. To exploit this, the teacher could create a slide presentation containing, for example, only text and pupils then adapt this adding sound and pictures from the files available on the computer. Another easy way to use PowerPoint is to create a series of slides to use as a gap-fill exercise or a form which pupils have to fill in.

- Provide a PowerPoint presentation in the target language, for example 'Healthy eating' or 'Visit our town'. Pupils then adapt this presentation, either to improve it, or to say the exact opposite!

- Learners who are confident with the multimedia features of PowerPoint can use it to produce a website with clickable links. Possible topics for such a website could be:
  - 'All about myself' – picture or title for each section with links to a short text about each area of writer's life.

- An electronic family tree – pictures of family members with links to information about each person.
- An electronic school brochure – a map of the school and pictures of the teachers link with descriptions of each.

WRITING IDEAS FOR SPREADSHEETS

• Use Excel or Word tables to create a timetable for a class (perhaps their real timetable). Allow them to use all of the edit facilities to alter it to their ideal timetable. This could include changing subjects, start and finish times, length of breaks, etc. A possible extension activity might be to write a few sentences justifying their choices, e.g. 'My favourite subject is …'; 'Our break is too short, so I want 45 minutes for break'.

• Use a spreadsheet to create a budget – perhaps as part of planning to go on holiday, on a trip, etc.

• Use a spreadsheet to carry out a comparison of prices in Great Britain and the target-language country. Use the functions to convert prices into Euros.

SUBJECT-SPECIFIC SOFTWARE FOR MFL WRITING

The generic software described above is now available on all PCs loaded with 'Windows'. In addition to this, you can buy software which is specifically designed to teach modern languages. Here are some of our favourites for encouraging writing.

FRENCH GRAMMAR STUDIO

French grammar studio is based on a series of photostories but also has a stand-alone programme for practising grammar skills. Learners construct the dialogue for the 'branching' photostories (see p49 for an explanation of 'branching' stories) using very tightly structured dialogue tables which allow a number of options. Pop-up help is available if errors are made and the completed photostory can be replayed as an audio-visual presentation. All eighteen photostories feature pictures of French teenagers in authentic settings and a particular strength is the way in which the learners' 'scripts' are read aloud immediately after they have written them, thus integrating the skills well. (Available in French only: www.granadalearning.co.uk)

WRITERS' WORKSHOP AND YOUNG WRITERS' WORKSHOP

Both these programs create situations in which young writers can take part in journalistic assignments that provoke stimulation for factual and imaginative writing. *Young writer's workshop* is suitable for KS3 (and younger depending on language proficiency), while *Writer's workshop* is more suitable for A level students. Users can incorporate video and audio clips as they script and record radio programmes and TV broadcasts. A 'language switch' allows learners to work in French, German and Spanish as well as English. (www.granadalearning.co.uk)

CiLT

FUN WITH TEXTS

This program is well known within the world of MFL ICT and has improved with age. It is easy for the teacher to use – the teacher just types in a source text which can range from a list of vocabulary to a long piece of prose. This text can now be turned into a variety of writing games, all of which require the leaner to reconstruct the source text. Can be used in a variety of languages. (www.camsoftpartners.co.uk)

WRITING FRAMES

The Folens *French frames for writing* series are all available on a CD-ROM version. The writing frame appears on-screen, supporting pupils as they write, but disappears when the completed text is printed out. The teacher can adapt the number of boxes and sentence starters. There is no limit on how much the learner can write, as the frame expands to accommodate whatever is written. Key vocabulary, link words and ideas are provided on-screen and these can be 'dragged and dropped' into the writing frame. (www.folens.com)

10. Encouraging reluctant writers

There is a great deal of writing for pupils to do at secondary school, and for children having difficulties with written language the amount of writing becomes a real problem; their written work is the visible evidence of failure and low standard. Such pupils will avoid writing, or produce very little. However, even the most reluctant pupil has something to say, and something to write. The main task is to put pen to paper, get started, and produce some work; at first, any written work is better than none. (Tainsh 1991: 3)

We agree wholeheartedly with Pam Tainsh's views. However, the context she was writing for was teachers of English as a mother tongue and in foreign language teaching we have added complications:

- Pupils are expected to write in a range of styles and areas in a context which is quite literally 'foreign' to them.
- The complexity of pupils' ideas usually exceeds the language they have available to express them.
- Reluctant writers are even less likely to write in a foreign language.

The ideas in previous chapters should be motivating, manageable and realistic for the majority of pupils, but we have collected here a few extra ideas which seem to encourage the most reluctant writers. The temptation with reluctant writers is to simplify the task, often opting for a utilitarian task, in a tourism or business context. However, these kinds of task are likely to prompt comments of 'But I'm not going to France anyway', or 'My dad says you don't need to be able to speak other languages to get a job'. So an alternative strategy is to opt for tasks which are intrinsically motivating because they are fun to do, genuinely interesting or relevant to the pupil, or have a wider purpose such as writing for an audience or competition.

Indeed, there is evidence that reluctant writers would respond better to creative, imaginative tasks. If a task involves paradox, irony or fantasy, it draws on the right side of the brain. This side of the brain is associated with creativity, divergent thinking, etc (McGee-Cooper 1990: 93).

LEFT BRAIN ◈	RIGHT BRAIN
logical	illogical
rational	irrational
facts	fantasy
knowledge	intuition
serious	playful
linear, sequential	holistic
2-D thinking	3-D thinking
book learning	common sense
monochronic time	polychronic time
creativity – implementation	creativity – 'aha'
pre-planning	spontaneous
structure, organisation	flexibility
'what's the bottom line?'	'have a heart'
algorithmic	heuristic

Source: McGee-Cooper (Bantam, 1990)

CiLT

This makes such tasks particularly suitable for reluctant writers who do not possess the skills associated with left-brained logical thinking. However, more usual writing tasks tend to focus on a linear convergent process, making them less accessible to reluctant writers, as Palmer describes here:

> *Poor writers often have difficulty organising their thoughts in order to write. Writing is essentially a linear process, requiring us to 'think in a straight line', which for many children does not come naturally. Preliminary planning can help – but non-linear thinkers may feel just as threatened by the traditional 'story plan' or 'essay plan' which also has a linear format.* (Palmer 2000: 13)

The following is a short extract from a Year 10 pupil, showing how he has used irony to describe the tiny Wiltshire village where he lives, using the format normally associated with describing a larger place:

> *Mon village s'appelle Leigh. Il y a une cabine téléphonique. Près de la cabine dans un champ il y a trente vaches et des moutons.* (James French, Bradon Forest School, Wiltshire)

ALTERNATIVES TO WRITING

Sometimes writing can be disguised as other activities. Throughout this Pathfinder we have illustrated ways to integrate writing with other skills, and incorporate writing into games. It is possible to take this idea one step further by using other means to create text.

'THE VELCRO GAME'

This game was invented by Rebecca Poole of Hendon School to practise the association of spoken and written forms in a motivating way and to improve spelling. Each group of pupils receives a board on which a strip of Velcro is stuck, plus a selection of letters with Velcro on the reverse. The teacher names a word and groups compete to see who can arrange the letters to spell out the word the most quickly. This game could also be played using different media – even pen and paper! However, Rebecca reports that pupils particularly enjoy the kinaesthetic element of individual letters with Velcro.

WRITING ACTIVITIES ON ICT

These can help to overcome an aversion to text – any activity with drag and drop tasks involving the rearrangement of text can be particularly productive. See Chapter 9 for further ideas on writing in an ICT context.

MAGNETIC POETRY

This can capture the attention of many pupils. It is particularly useful for tactile learners who learn best through touching and moving things. Magnetic poetry is now available in English, French, German, Spanish, Italian, Yiddish and Sign Language. Each kit comes with a mini-dictionary and blank magnets to add words of your own. Visit **www.magneticpoetry.com** to see the materials and play the game on-line.

Using this item which might be familiar from their lives outside school would particularly motivate some learners. This idea would be easy to replicate with pieces of paper (on p11 we suggest a writing game where the pupils prepare all of the pieces of paper!).

MOTIVATING TASKS FOR RELUCTANT WRITERS

It is not surprising the 'long tail of underachievement' in writing is worse than in reading. To write, they must orchestrate a wide range of skills and knowledge (wielding a pen, matching sounds to symbols, dealing with spelling rules and irregularities ...) and generate ideas at the same time (dreaming up content, seeking words to express it, organising them into sentences and paragraphs to make sense to the reader ...). If they are at a loss in one or more of these areas, the whole enterprise can come crashing to a halt. (Palmer 2000: 12)

One of the key features of motivating reluctant writers is finding a task where they are genuinely motivated to write. In a recent piece of research about GCSE coursework, one teacher told a story of two boys who had already been signed up as apprentice footballers and weren't remotely interested in their MFL studies:

... they were both slightly disaffected, they were into their football basically, and I convinced them if they were to come to the lesson and do the coursework, that they would pass and they would get some sort of a grade ... One of the [coursework tasks] we did was 'Am I fit?' so that fitted in nicely with 'I play football' and 'I've got big muscles'! They enjoyed writing about their physique and how fit they were so that was again motivation for them. (Adams 2000a: 14)

PUBLISHING WRITING

In this section we leave aside the issue of 'what' to write and 'how' to teach pupils to write it, to focus briefly on the issue of presenting pupils' writing. Very often, an attractive presentation format can be enough to get some pupils writing. Book making might strike a particular chord with pupils, as it is an activity they will be familiar with from primary school. This particular method of making a book was sent to us by Stephen Clare and is actually very simple (see opposite). However, when we have used it at INSET sessions, we have discovered that most teachers are 'origamically challenged'! If you do everything correctly, you should end up with a book with eight pages numbered in the correct order. If your book doesn't work, follow the instructions carefully, and ask an eight-year old to help you!

CILT

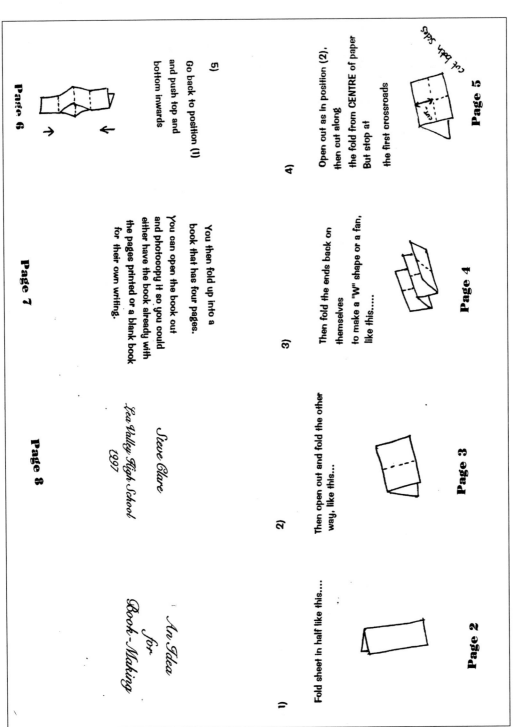

Page 5

4) Open out as in position (2), then cut along the fold from CENTRE of paper But stop at the first crossroads

cut both sides

Page 6

5) Go back to position (1) and push top and bottom inwards

Page 4

3) Then fold the ends back on themselves to make a "W" shape or a fan, like this.....

Page 7

You then fold up into a book that has four pages.

You can open the book out and photocopy it so you could either have the book already with the pages printed or a blank book for their own writing.

Page 3

2) Then open out and fold the other way, like this...

Page 2

1) Fold sheet in half like this....

Page 8

Steve Clare
Lea Valley High School
1997

An Idea for Book-Making

Source: Stephen Clare, Lea Valley High School

This is a similar idea from Ann Phillips, St John Lloyd School, Llanelli.

INSTRUCTIONS for making a house

1. Fold A4 paper half lengthways.

2. Open paper out and fold each half

3. Open out again and fold whole paper in half the other way (widthways).

Open out.

4. Fold one short end towards middle.

5. Fold sides into middle again.

6. Fold top 2 corners down to form a roof (the folds form the different rooms).

The usefulness of such presentation formats is that they effectively challenge pupils to write something in each box or on every page. If you enjoy creative practical ideas like this, you will find the following books valuable for further stimulus ideas: *Making books: A step-by-step guide to your own publishing* (Chapman and Robson, 1995). See also: *Words with wings: Ideas for writing in different forms and contexts* (Andrew 1991) and *On course for GCSE coursework* (Adams 1998: 10) for other ideas of pictorial structure for writing tasks.

Publishing pupils' work (even in a very simple format) helps increase motivation to write. For example, compile poems from everyone in the class into an anthology – you only need a hole punch and a spare ring binder to do this – and ask for a volunteer to make a title page. If pupils are working on similar role-plays in a transactional topic, collate their work together afterwards and present it as a phrasebook for that topic. For example, Maggie Fernandes of The Edgware School in Barnet prepared pupils to write a shopping dialogue. They were given a standard format to use or adapt, with 'menus' of alternative shops and shopping items. The pupils wrote in pairs and word-processed their dialogues. Afterwards Maggie collected together all printouts and bound them as a 'phrasebook'. Such phrasebooks or anthologies could be used just for display purposes, or shown to other classes as a reading task. It is surprising how willing pupils are to read through 30 very similar accounts of 'My favourite food and drink', for example, if they know they have been written by pupils from another class! Alternatively, the compilations of similar dialogues can be used to help pupils to revise, as they show clearly how language models can be adapted in differing contexts.

cilt

WRITING IN GROUPS

The secretarial skills – handwriting and spelling – are important, but composition is even more crucial. Writing is a social process. Frank Smith (1982), for instance, talks in terms of creating an atmosphere in schools and classroom which is akin to a 'literary club' which all children, when motivated by an enthusiastic adult, will want to join. (Edwards 1995: 2)

Throughout this Pathfinder we have suggested ways of getting pupils to write in groups. Iain Mitchell has used this idea of writing as a 'club' by organising pupils to write a newspaper (see p66). This contained sections on interviews with German speakers in the school, cartoon strips, whose birthday is when, results of various surveys, tourist tips for their own town, poems, report on exchange trip, quizzes, 'You've won €1000 – what would you buy?', letters to the editor, small ads. This is a good way to join together several small pieces of writing into a larger result. We anticipate that this is a piece of work that pupils would be likely to be proud of and keep. The variety of articles in the newspaper made it easy to provide differentiated tasks and also allowed pupils some choice in what they were going to write about.

While there are activities which lend themselves very well to writing in groups, it is also possible to use more ordinary tasks as group work. Rebecca Fontecilla, then of Willesden High School in Brent, often organised her pupils into pairs and small groups for 'everyday' writing tasks:

This actually worked rather well as a pairwork activity because it worked out that you had a higher achiever working with a lower achiever in some cases ... the higher achiever tended to be the scribe, but as I was going around monitoring I did notice that some of the lower achievers were thinking of the ideas, so although they weren't necessarily doing the writing, in that particular case they were contributing ideas, which was good.

When encouraging writing in groups, the teacher can model this process, by scribing the text, taking ideas from pupils. This also gives pupils some text to critique. Sue Palmer recommends giving a 'running commentary' on:

- *what you plan to say (oral rehearsal of sentences before writing);*
- *the choices you make and the ways you edit as you compose;*
- *the way you read through regularly to check it sounds right.*

She concludes that 'all pupils benefit from this sort of explicit talk about writing, but poor writers benefit most of all' (Palmer 2000: 13).

Finally, a surprising piece of advice about reluctant writers: **you** must raise your expectations of the standard of learners' work. Often the least able are given obviously trivial and undemanding tasks. Realising this, pupils put little or no effort into such tasks. As long as there is good preparation, support and a **meaningful** task, nearly all learners can engage in worthwhile writing.

Geisterbahn

10p   Zeitung von 2msh   20pf

DEUTSCHE IN ERNULF

Vier Deutsche arbeiten in Ernulf. Sie sind Swantje Rickers, die Assistentin, Herr Haubert ein Lehrer, Klaus Kellert in 1JS und Kai Schell in 2AB. Sie sprechen mit Shelley Gardner und Rosalyn Bardsley

SWANTJE RICKERS

Sie heißt Swantje Rickers. Sie wohnt in Cambridge. Sie hat einen Bruder und zwei Schwestern. Sie hat eine Katze und einen Hund. Sie ist am dreiundzwanzigsten März geboren. Sie spielt Volleyball. Sie ißt zum Frühstück Muesli und sie trinkt Kaffee um sieben Uhr. Sie wohnt in Deutschland sechsundzwanzig Jahre; sie wohnt in England sie weiß nicht! Sie findet England sehr schön!

HERR HAUBERT

Er heißt Hermann Haubert. Er wohnt in Cambridge aber er kommt aus Deutschland. Er hat zwei Schwestern, die eine ist fünfunddreißig und die andere ist sechsundzwanzig. Seine Haustiere sind ein Hund, ein Wellensittich und ein Zebrafink! Er hat am achten August Geburtstag. Er ißt zum Frühstück Müsli und er trinkt Kaffee um Viertel nach sieben. Er geht gern ins Kino, Konzerte, und er spielt Badminton und er geht zum Tanzklub. Er sagt, England ist sehr gut und Deutschland ist sehr schön. Er wohnt zwei Jahre in England.

KAI SCHELL

Er heißt Kai Schell. Er wohnt in Eaton Socon. Er hat eine Schwester, sie ist heißt Katja. Er hat zwei Hamsters, ein Meerschweinchen, ein Kaninchen und vier Goldfische. Er hat Geburtstag am dreizehnten August. Er spielt Fußball. Er ißt Honey Smacks und trinkt Orangensaft zum Frühstück um halb sechs.

KLAUS KELLET

Er heißt Klaus Thomas Kellett und er wohnt in 25 Queens Gardens, Eaton Socon. Klaus hat eine Schwester und sie heißt Jenny und sie ist sechs Jahre alt. Er hat drei Meerschweinchen und er ist zwölf im Juni. Er ißt zum Frühstück Cornflakes und er trinkt Wasser um sechs Uhr! Er spielt gern in der Freizeit. Er wohnt zwei Jahre in England und er sagt "England ist gut aber Deutschland ist besser!"

CILT

11.   Teaching writing in a new script

Tackling the issue of non-Roman scripts is vital if we are to expand the uptake of these languages. Unfortunately languages with different scripts tend to reinforce the notion of 'separateness' from English. (John Ferguson, ALL Language World Conference 30.6.00)

The report of the Nuffield Languages Inquiry recommends that more money should be put into schools to support the teaching of Chinese, Japanese, Arabic and Russian. All these languages, in addition to the usual challenges of learning a foreign language, require Western Europeans to learn a new script. A myth exists that languages with different scripts are beyond the capabilities of all but the most able children, but Viv Edwards supports our view that: 'Children are often enthusiastic about the chance to learn other scripts' (Edwards 1995: 18). In fact, some teachers believe that teaching a new script is one way to improve handwriting and approach 'reading rescue'. Even Chinese, for example, can be well within the grasp of a secondary pupil if taught well.

A debate currently exists among teachers of languages with non-Roman scripts about the best way to tackle the teaching of writing. The traditional approach has always been to teach the alphabet – in strict alphabetical order – and only to proceed to more complex (and therefore more interesting) writing tasks when the individual letters have been fully mastered. However, many teachers feel that it is more productive and motivating to go from meaning to form, by teaching whole words first and then working 'backwards' to individual letters.

John Ferguson, Chair of ALL's Asian Languages Committee, feels strongly that in teaching writing with another script, we are not teaching a mental discipline, but are providing learners with a tool. He feels we need to get learners interested in the written script by getting them reading. This reflects practice in KS1, where children are introduced to whole words and real books in their mother tongue, and learn individual letters on a 'need-to-know' basis. On the other hand, it must be pointed out that the National Literacy Strategy advocates a return to the inclusion of phonics as one element of teaching reading. Therefore, a sensible mid-way might be to adopt an approach which covers both methods. In the *100 word exercise book* series, the introduction explains to learners:

> *Many of the activities are inspired by the kind of games used to teach children to read their own language: flashcards, matching games, memory games, joining exercise, etc. This is not only a more effective method of learning to read a new script, but also more fun.* (Wightwick 1999: 4)

The activities described above are also part of the standard repertoire of any modern foreign language teacher and can be used in virtually any language. In Russian and Greek, where there is a fairly consistent correlation between the letter and the sound it represents when read aloud, it can be very helpful to work at the level of individual letters. However, in scripts such as written Arabic, where letters are modified once they are included in words, it seems to make more sense to teach whole words rather than 'notional' letters which don't actually exist once they are included in a word. We do not have a fixed view of which method is best, but feel certain that a combination of approaches and wide variety of activities and what Edwards describes as 'extended exposure to the written language and opportunities to experiment' (Edwards 1999: 17) will allow for all learning styles.

> *Remember that recognising the whole shape of the word in an unfamiliar script is just as important as knowing how it is made up. Using this method you will have a much more instinctive recall of vocabulary and will gain the confidence to expand your knowledge in other directions.* (Wightwick 1995: 5)

PRACTICAL IDEAS FOR TEACHING A NEW SCRIPT

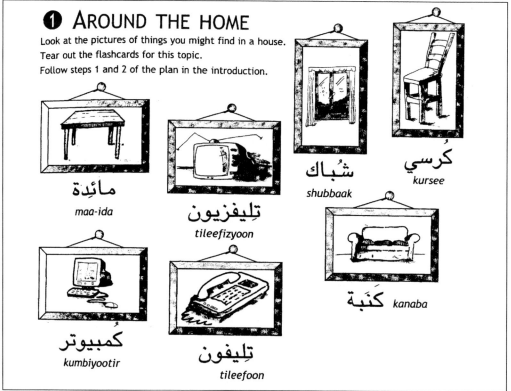

① AROUND THE HOME

Look at the pictures of things you might find in a house.
Tear out the flashcards for this topic.
Follow steps 1 and 2 of the plan in the introduction.

مَائِدة
maa-ida

تِليفزيون
tileefizyoon

شُبَّاك
shubbaak

كُرسي
kursee

كَنَبة *kanaba*

كُمبيوتر
kumbiyootir

تِليفون
tileefoon

Source: Wightwick (GW Publishing, 1999)

Materials for teaching the script to native-speaker young children tend not to appeal to children of secondary age, being illustrated with various cuddly animals, childish toys or unknown cultural references. Instead, it is better to use those materials (or create your own) specifically designed for teaching the language as a foreign or second language, such as the Arabic example shown above. For example, instead of 'a is for apple, b is for ball, etc' allow pupils to build up their own alphabet, where each letter is represented by a word they have learnt or chosen, e.g. B is for BphqlhÐ Qnhpc (answer on p80).

CiLT

Peter Reznikov of Eton College has adapted this alphabet chart from pictures in a book aimed at (native-speaker) Russian children learning to read. It shows a picture for each letter of the alphabet, but the picture takes the shape of the letter it represents. For example, K is for Kangaroo, and the picture of the kangaroo is (roughly) the shape of a letter K.

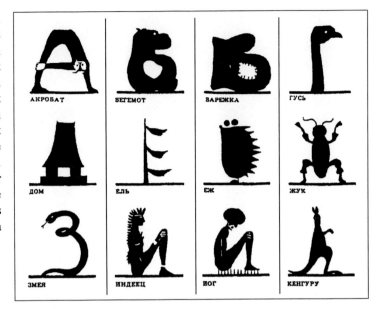

Children (and adult learners!) take a great deal of pleasure in learning to write their names in a new script. Here, Hannah has used Japanese Hiragana, Katakana and Kanji to write her name (Ha-na), providing a starting point in her understanding of the various Japanese writing systems.

Hiragana

Katakana

Kanji

If you are a fluent user of the writing system you are trying to teach, it is easy to overlook features which you take for granted. One of the frequent questions that pupils ask when learning Cyrillic, for example, is whether Russians use full stops and commas 'like in English'. This checklist of features you have to consider when teaching to write in a different script might be a helpful prompt in teaching the script to beginners:

- size of letters;
- printed/handwritten script in upper/lower case;
- diacritics and accents;
- positioning on the line;
- direction of writing;
- (non-)representation of vowels;
- position of vowels;
- letter change according to position;
- hooks on letters.

Bengali letters 'hanging off' the line

আজ ঈদ   (Today is Eid)

এই আমার বই   (This is my book)

MORE IDEAS FOR TEACHING LETTERS

- Create a reference chart for pupils' own books, with helpful equivalent sounds (those in many coursebooks are incomprehensible to KS3 pupils!).

- When teaching a new script letter by letter, it is not necessary to teach all the letters at once. Similarly, teach letters in the order of frequency/usefulness, rather than in alphabetical order.

- As an early homework, ask all pupils to draw one letter as large as they can on a sheet of A4 paper. Use to create an alphabet frieze for the classroom. Repeat this homework until you have a frieze for upper and lower case alphabets in both handwritten and printed forms (there are inevitably more letters than pupils, but there are equally inevitably volunteers to do extra letters).

- Encourage games which involve guessing the shape of the letters, e.g. by tracing with a finger on the OHP, tracing the letter on your partner's back, or tracing the shape in the air

- Associate a silly noise with each stroke (e.g. a speeding car noise for curves, a whoosh for upward strokes, a boom for a downward stroke) and practise 'air writing' with the appropriate sound accompaniment.

- Emphasise the similarities, e.g. aекоqg in Russian (the letters which make up ïkeqa!), or letters they will know from other contexts Π and Ω in Greek, CCCP in Russian.

- Use international words, brand names, sport, names of cities, countries and famous people, etc.

- Teach the lower handwritten case first, as this is the one they will use most often in their own writing.

- Update the slate traditionally used in Koran schools with an Etch-a-Sketch, Magic Slate toy (reusable plastic writing sheet), or mini-whiteboards. The advantage of these over paper is that learners feel confident they can erase any errors. Also, these larger formats allow learners to draw the letters very large, helping the development of the kinaesthetic sense (this idea also works for whole words).

- Introduce printed typefaces as a 'discovery' activity where pupils find the matches themselves – point out how different the handwritten and printed 'g' are in English.

- In Arabic, make use of the characters used as abbreviations of common words such as *alif* for *abu* (dad), *ba* for *bab* (door), and so on.

MORE IDEAS FOR TEACHING WORDS

- Generate learners' interest in the new written form by displaying posters, notices, packaging, carrier bags and older pupils' work containing the new script.

- Ask older pupils to prepare pictures of famous people with their names written in the new script, e.g. O ow QnaÐc, Bassh baкnhp cɟÐep (answers on p80).

ciLT

- Use listening as input for reading – allow pupils to read a word at the same time as they hear it spoken. Again, older pupils can record onto cassette some of the sentences and short texts in the coursebook, or others specially written for this purpose such as older pupils introducing themselves.

- Teach reading initially if you are using the whole-word approach and leave writing until later.

- In Arabic, teach words in groups where they all share the same root/trace, for example, *ba, ta, tha, fa, qaf* and so on. This helps learners distinguish words that differ from each other only by the diacritical signs (dots under or over the letter).

MORE IDEAS FOR TEACHERS OF PICTOGRAMIC WRITTEN FORMS

- Insist that learners always write the strokes in the same order, as they are then less likely to omit a brush stroke in a fixed sequence of strokes. Also, the kinaesthetic sense they develop when they write the word in the same way each time will help learners to remember it.

- Introduce learners to the imitative or indicative schematic 'pictures' of real objects or abstract concepts. The pictures here show how the original picture was changed into *Kanji* (Gilhooly 1999: 3).

Look at the following artist's impression of the sequence of progressive changes, from standardised 漢字 (*kanji*) character back to original picture.

漢字 (*kanji*) Character	絵 (*e*) Picture	英語 (*eigo*) English
山	山 → 山 → ⌒ → ⌂	mountain
川	川 → 川 → 彳	river
金	金 → 金 → 𐂃 → ⌂	gold/money
田	田 → 田 → 艸	rice field
竹	竹 → 竹 → 竹 → 竹	bamboo
火	火 → 火 → 火	fire
木	木 → 木 → 木	tree

Source: Gilhooly (Hodder & Stoughton, 1999)

- Invent mnemonics which help learners to remember the shapes and sounds of the *hiragana* by linking them to visual and audio stimuli. Here are examples for the first five sounds 'a, i, u, e, o' taken from *Teach yourself beginners' Japanese script* (Gilhooly 1999). The first, for example, shows an opera singer singing an aria, to represent the 'ah' sound!

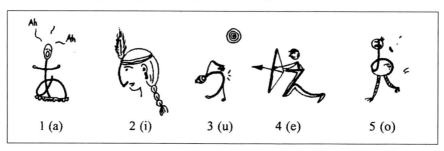

Source: Gilhooly (Hodder & Stoughton, 1999)

PUPILS BILINGUAL IN A COMMUNITY LANGUAGE

Speakers of community languages are likely to have an excellent level in speaking and listening, but may never have learnt to read or write at all in this language. Alternatively they might have learnt to read the language in religious instruction, but the form and register will be very different to the one they speak (and therefore the one we would expect them to use in examinations). Many bilingual children will therefore experience difficulties with the mismatch in their skill levels and might even be resistant to learning the written form. In this case, it is important to boost their confidence by assuring them of how much they already can do and adopting some of the methods suggested above which emphasise the similarity and accessibility of the new written form. Edwards particularly recommends 'Process writing' which we discussed in Chapter 2:

> *Process writing – whether or not in the context of workshops – is supportive of the writing development of all children. However, it is particularly helpful in the case of bilingual children for two main reasons. First, the opportunity to rehearse ideas, vocabulary and structures provides a valuable boost to children's confidence. Second, this approach has the potential to reduce children's anxiety and to encourage risk taking. Because children are not expected to produce perfect copy at the first attempt, process writing can help alleviate the sense of failure which bilingual learners often feel when their writing is 'corrected'.* (Edwards 1995: 7)

While there are increasing numbers of bilingual children's books available, these are not always the favourites or the most up-to-date books. So, as a writing task with a real audience, pupils can be supported to write their own bilingual books for younger learners. Bilingual learners are more likely to have knowledge of the appropriate vocabulary, having themselves (usually) learnt the language as children. They could be particularly encouraged to write a bilingual version of their own favourite children's book.

C*i*LT

12.   Marking and assessment of writing

Correctness of writing is more than a matter of practice – it is essentially a matter of responsibility. Teachers who offer to correct their students' written work without insisting on the students themselves checking it thoroughly are not only adding considerably to their already heavy workload – they are also doing their students positive harm ... It is only when students develop this sense of responsibility that they will be capable of writing [the target language] without numerous, unnecessary mistakes. (Jupp and Milne 1980: 11)

MARKING OF WRITING

One of the questions we encounter at INSET sessions is about marking: 'If we are giving pupils all this written work, doesn't that increase the amount of marking we have to do?'

One easy solution to this is to teach pupils to mark their own work! In Chapter 6 we discussed how to encourage pupils to edit their own work. This, traditionally, has always been one of the reasons why we mark work – to identify all of the errors so that pupils can copy up a perfect version. (This begs the questions – Copy it up where? What for?) If we correct all of the errors for pupils, this means that they do not have to think about their own writing. One way to teach pupils how to edit or mark their own work is to copy one pupil's work onto an overhead transparency and to look at the piece of writing as a whole class. Ideas are also given for improving the piece of writing – it has been our experience that when pupils have seen a written draft enhanced in this way, many then volunteer to have their work marked by the whole class.

Even if you feel nervous about asking pupils to assess their own writing as we suggest below, you could at least ask them to take responsibility for their own corrections. To do this, you will need to annotate their work in a way pupils will understand. You could make use of the common abbreviations used for this purpose such as 'sp' for spelling. Draw up a list of such annotations at a departmental meeting (if your school does not already have such a policy) and display them in each languages classroom. After each piece of writing is returned allocate a small amount of time – and appropriate support materials – for making corrections. In the past we might automatically have changed any incorrect articles, for example, but using this system, you would draw pupils' attention to the fact that the article is wrong and they then work out for themselves whether they need to change the gender, or change it to an in-/definite article. Pupils' own corrections might not always be correct, but at least they will be thinking about their writing.

It is clearly neither motivating nor conducive to learning to identify every single mistake on a pupil's piece of writing, but what then can we do instead? Is it OK to leave errors uncorrected? Not only is it acceptable, we suggest it is educationally advisable to target only certain errors. One approach we have used with success is 'focus' marking, that is concentrating on just one or two areas for correction in each text. For example, if you have recently been working on the perfect tense, when you mark the next piece of written work, you could focus only on the errors that are part of that language area.

However, we might inadvertently be giving the impression that you should only mark for errors! Despite the amounts of red ink we enthusiastically lavish on pupils' work, very little of it is used for praise. In fact, pointing out which parts of the text are good is often a better way to help some writers improve and fits in well with some modern approaches to behaviour management – catch them doing something right and praise them for it! Items singled out for praise could include:

- an interesting idea;
- opinion;
- justification of opinions;
- good use of tenses;
- ambitious vocabulary;

- detailed descriptions;
- humour (intentional!);
- coverage of required content;
- content which goes beyond the prescribed task.

One question which MFL teachers have to ask every time they mark a learner's piece of work is which language any comments should be written in. Harmer Parr gives two helpful replies to this question:

> *Firstly, if something important needs to be said and that something would be incomprehensible in the target language, say it in English. Secondly, explore ways of making more comments understood in the target language.* (Parr 1997: 5)

Following Parr's logic it is clear that sometimes we need to give feedback in English if we are to help pupils improve their writing, and a numerical grade does not achieve this.

We should look upon the assessment of pupils' written work as another opportunity to create 'real' writing opportunities with an authentic audience. Before we, the teachers, start to mark pupils' work, we could use it as an opportunity for pupils to reflect on their own learning and write about this. This is not difficult to achieve, even for beginners. If the pupils are introduced to a set of stock phrases for describing their own work, they can comment on their own progress.

En cet exercice d'écriture, j'ai _____ travaillé.	(bien/assez bien)
Je l'ai trouvé _____.	(difficile/facile/intéressant/ennuyeux)
Pour améliorer je peux _____.	(écrire plus/apprendre mon vocabulaire ...)

ASSESSMENT OF WRITING

> *Despite the fact that it is acknowledged that writing is a difficult skill for many pupils to acquire, it is often used as a convenient, though often inappropriate, means of assessing the other skills. In terms of assessment, as Rivers pointed out 25 years ago, teachers are often harshest on pupils in writing activities, the testimony for this being red-ink-spattered exercise books.* (Swarbrick 1994: 142)

Marking and assessing pupils' written work takes up a large amount of the teacher's time, therefore we need to be sure that we are using this time as productively as possible. In most schools there are now effective marking policies which require teachers to report on each piece of work for both effort and attainment, for example. These can be usefully adopted by MFL teachers. However, all too often such markschemes deflect us from helping pupils to see how they could improve their work, not just what their current level of attainment is.

Most pieces of writing can be assessed very effectively by looking at just two criteria:

- How much has been communicated? (content/communication)
- How clearly has it been communicated? (accuracy/use of language)

Content/communication is arguably the most important element of the two: in the exam context the marks awarded for content can limit the maximum amount of marks available for use of language and accuracy. However, this is a difficult message to get across, as pupils must not sacrifice accuracy and fluency for the sake of increased **amounts** of content – **quality** of content is also a factor. Therefore, our feedback on pupils' written work should address both of these points.

With training and practice, pupils can even be asked to assess their own writing, with teachers acting mainly as 'moderators'. For this to be successful, pupils will need to understand:

- the markscheme and/or NC levels;
- the objectives of the task;
- what standards are expected.

These points are all parts of best practice in making pupils understand better the purpose of their work and how well they are achieving – and why. In order to communicate these points to pupils, we need to be sure about them ourselves. The GCSE coursework process requires that teachers across the department standardise their marking. Although regarded by some as a time-wasting inconvenience, these discussions can be an important point of professional sharing, understanding and progress. It is such discussions and the ensuing decisions which form the basis for an assessment policy.

Pupils can be encouraged to assess their own writing using 'pupil-friendly' renditions of the NC levels.

Level 1
I can copy words and short phrases that I know. I can choose the correct word to complete a sentence.

This is a continuation of the drafting and editing process described in Chapter 6, and ideally should be tackled even before pupils submit their final draft. At the redrafting stage of writing, tell pupils what they would need to do to reach the next level in

Level 5
I can write short pieces of writing. I can ask and answer questions and give opinions. I can write in the present tense and include another tense in my writing. Other people can understand my writing easily. I can use a dictionary to check words and look up new words.

writing, and then encourage them to add to their text accordingly.

Increasing pupils' understanding of the success criteria in this way should help them if not to improve their writing then at least to understand why they have been awarded a particular grade.

Conclusion

We hope we have shown that writing is a skill suitable for learners of all levels of attainment and an integral part of learning a foreign language, rather than a 'bolt-on' activity at the end of a unit. There have been several recurring themes throughout this Pathfinder, which offer a model for teachers to follow, namely:

- Writing is integrated with the other skills.

- Writing is not left until the end of the unit, but used as a learning tool in itself.

- Learners are given a thorough and active introduction to new written forms which helps to associate them clearly with the spoken form of the language.

- New symbols and letters are introduced actively and imaginatively.

- Writing tasks are often rehearsed orally before starting to write.

- Learners regularly see the teacher writing and the teacher often acts as the scribe for pupils' ideas.

- Learners are given support for their writing – in vocabulary, suggestions for content and the structure of the text.

- Pupils are given opportunities to look analytically at the writing of others.

- Writing tasks are varied and often have an audience.

- Even simple writing tasks should involve some element of thought/choice/selection/discrimination.

- Writing takes place in a variety of formats (not just pen and paper).

- Pupils are taught explicit writing skills, including editing and drafting.

- Writing tasks take account of the range of learning styles.

- Ambitious creative tasks are included regularly.

- Writing tasks are used to expand knowledge of the culture and other meaningful content.

- Effective writers build up a portfolio of their writing.

- Writing tasks are sometimes carried out in pairs and groups.

- Writing is not always treated as a test.

- Feedback on writing is often positive and always formative.

- Pupils are involved in assessing their own writing.

It is obviously not possible to incorporate all of these features into every writing task, but an effective and imaginative teacher would seek to cover most of these areas with his/her class. We leave the final word to Ellis and Friel:

> *It is clear that successful writers believe that the ideas they write down are important. They know why they are writing and who is likely to read them. They have thought about how best to express their ideas so that the reader will understand ... In short, successful writers are driven by a sense of purpose and a sense of audience.* (Ellis and Friel 1991: 6)

References

Adams J, *On course for GCSE coursework* (CILT, 1998)

Adams J, 'Raising standards in MFL writing through coursework' in *Studies in Modern Languages Education,* Vol 8, April 2000 (University of Leeds, 2000*a*)

Adams J, *French writing frames 11–14: Creative and imaginative writing* and *Personal feelings and opinions* (other titles available in the series) (Folens, 2000*b*)

Andrew M, *Words with wings: Ideas for writing in different forms and contexts* (Belair, 1991)

Beard R (ed), *Rhyme, reading and writing* (Hodder & Stoughton, 1995)

Berwick G and S Thorne, *Mach mit!* (Nelson Thornes, 2001)

Bourdais D, S Finnie and A L Gordon, *Équipe 4* (OUP, 2000)

Brownjohn S, 'Rhyme in children's writing', Chapter 5 in Beard, *op cit* (1995)

Bruzzone C and L Morton, *Pen pals: A friendship in French and English* (b small publishing, 1998)

Buckby M and T Huntley (eds), *Auto 1* (Collins Educational, 1992)

Byrne D, *Teaching writing skills* (Longman, 1998)

Chapman G and P Robson, *Making books: A step-by-step guide to your own publishing* (Macdonald Young Books, 1995)

Clark A, *Gender on the agenda* (CILT, 1998)

Crossland D and P Horsfall, *Key to French writing skills* (*The Key to GCSE* series) (John Murray Publishing, 1998)

Edwards V, *Writing in multilingual classrooms* (University of Reading: Reading and Language Information Centre, 1995)

Ellis S and G Friel G, *Inspirations for writing* (Scholastic, 1991)

Elston T, P McLagan and A Swarbrick, *Génial 1* (OUP, 1995)

Fowler M, 'Developing writing skills' in Littlewood W (ed), *Developing modern language skills for GCSE:* 90–115 (Thomas Nelson, 1989)

Gilhooly H, *Teach yourself beginners' Japanese script* (Hodder & Stoughton, 1999)

Gläsmann S and M Calvert, *Tandem language learning in schools* (Philip Armstrong Publications, 2000)

Hares R, *Teach yourself GCSE French* (Hodder & Stoughton, 1987)

Hawkins E, *Modern languages in the curriculum* (CUP, 1981)

HMI, *Modern foreign languages to 16: Curriculum matters 8* (HMSO, 1987)

Jupp T C and J Milne, *Basic writing skills in English: Teacher's handbook* (Heinemann Educational Books, 1980)

Kavanagh B and L Upton, Pathfinder 21: *Creative use of texts* (CILT, 1994)

Lee J, D Buckland and G Shaw, *The invisible child* (CILT, 1998)

McColl H, *Modern languages for all* (David Fulton Publishers, 2000)

McColl H with S Thomas, *Ici on parle francais: French for beginners* (Miniflashcard Language Games, 1997)

McGee-Cooper A with D Trammell and B Lau, *You don't have to go home from work exhausted!* (New York: Bantam, 1990)

Morris P and A Wesson, *Lernpunkt Deutsch 1* (Thomas Nelson, 1996)

Palmer S, 'Can't write, won't write?' in *TES Curriculum Special* (Spring 2000)

Parr H, Pathfinder 29: *Assessment and planning in the MFL department* (CILT, 1997)

Raithby K and A Taylor, *Creative Key Stage 4 French* (MLG Publishing, 2001)

Rogers P, L Briggs, B Goodman-Stephens and H Seeger, *Zickzack neu 4* (Thomas Nelson, 1996)

Schenk C, *Hands on: Hands off – a computer activity book for schools* (A & C Black, 1986)

Swarbrick A, *Teaching modern languages* (Routledge/Open University, 1994)

Swarbrick A, M Calvert and A L Gordon, *ALL French writing activities for KS4* (Association for Language Learning, 1997)

Tainsh P, *Encouraging writing* (Folens, 1991)

Whitrod S et al, *Guidelines to literacy teaching* (PRU Publications, 1982)

Wightwick J, *The 100 word exercise book* (available in Arabic, Chinese, Greek, Japanese Russian and Urdu) (GW Publishing, 1999)

Notes

SECRET AGENT • P15

Hello my name is Secret Agent X

RUSSIAN POEM • P19

V ponedyelnik – mandarin
On Monday, a mandarine
A vo vtornik – apyelsin
But on Tuesday, an orange
V sredoo – shokolad
On Wednesday, chocolate
V chetverg – marmelad
On Thursday, jelly
V pyatnitsoo – vinograd
On Friday, grapes
V soobottoo – pecheniye
On Saturday, a biscuit
V voskresenye – varenye
On Sunday, jam

RHYMING COUPLETS • P21

Je m'appelle Clément, j'ai mal aux dents.
Florence étudie les sciences.
L'éléphant est marrant.

TEACHING WRITERS' SKILLS • P33

Aller Anfang ist schwer. – Getting started is always difficult.
C'est le premier pas qui compte. – it's the first step that counts.
A journey of a thousand miles begins with a single step.

千里之行
始於足下

TEACHING A NEW SCRIPT • P68

B is for Britney Spears

MORE IDEAS FOR TEACHING WORDS • P70

Posh Spice, Buffy the Vampire Slayer

GAP-FILL TEXT • P36

1 = und • The best word here is *und* to join two similar ideas.
2 = aber • The best word here is *aber* to join two contrasting ideas, although *und* would also make sense.
3 = aber • The best word here is *aber* to join two contrasting ideas, although *und* would also make sense.
4 = vielleicht • The best word here is *vielleicht* to give the meaning of 'perhaps'.
5 = Zuerst • The best word here is *zuerst* because Carl is starting to describe a list of things that happened to him.
6 = dann • The best word here is *dann* because Carl is in the middle of describing a list of things that happened to him.
7 = weil • The best word here is *weil*, and notice how it has sent the verb to the end.
8 = auch • The best word here is *auch* because Carl is describing something else that he would like to do.
9 = um ... zu • The best answer here is *um ... zu* because Carl is giving a reason why it would be a good idea to go to Germany – in order to improve his German.
10 = aber • The best word here is *aber* to join two contrasting ideas.
11 = nur • The best word here is *nur*, to emphasise that he has only saved a bit of money.

CILT